P9-DOE-970

THE GLORY OF CHRIST

THE
GLORY
OF
CHRIST
RC SPROUL

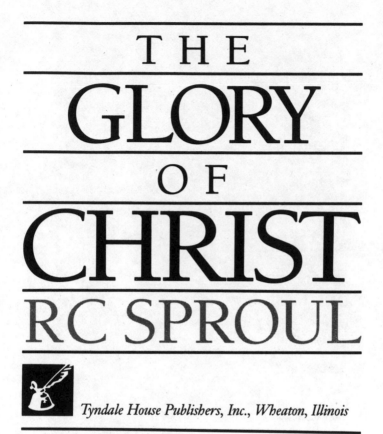

Tyndale House Publishers, Inc., Wheaton, Illinois

Front cover illustration: Michael Hackett

Unless otherwise noted, scripture quotations are from the *Holy Bible,*
New International Version. Copyright © 1973, 1978, 1984 International
Bible Society. Used by permission of Zondervan Bible Publishers.
Verses marked NKJV are from *The New King James Version.* Copyright
© 1979, 1980, 1982, Thomas Nelson Inc., Publishers.

Library of Congress Catalog Card Number 90-70613
ISBN 0-8423-1041-X
Copyright © 1990 by R. C. Sproul
All rights reserved
Printed in the United States of America

96 95 94 93 92 91 90
 9   8   7   6   5   4   3   2   1

For RALPH VEERMAN,
DAVID FOX,
and ROBERT INGRAM,
my comrades and fellow laborers in Christ

CONTENTS

PREFACE

Glory. The word is charged with meaning. It sets the hearts of Christians soaring. The soul is lifted up by the contemplation of the glory of God and of His Only Begotten Son. It is Christ in His glory who is the object of our worship and adoration. As Christians we join the communion of saints and the host of heaven in lifting up praise and honor to Him.

Jesus' life was marked by humiliation and suffering. His humanity served as a veil that concealed the splendor of His deity. Yet there were moments when His glory shone through. It was as if the vessel of His human nature was not strong enough to conceal it at all times.

There is a Latin phrase that was popular among sixteenth-century theologians: *finitum non capax infinitum.* The phrase conveyed two ideas. The first was that the finite cannot grasp the infinite. In this sense it calls attention to the incomprehensibility of God. It points to the limits of our human minds to grasp fully the greatness of God. At our best our understanding of Him is feeble.

The second idea the Latin phrase conveyed was that the finite cannot *contain* the infinite. So it was in the incarnation. Though the fullness of the Godhead dwelt in Christ bodily, it could not be restricted to His human nature nor held in subjection by it.

This book is not intended to provide a full examination of the life of Jesus. Rather, it focuses on moments in Jesus' life when His glory burst forth and was displayed to those around Him. It considers those points where His humiliation gave way to exaltation.

Whenever I write a book I like to give the proper acknowledgments to those who helped in the process. In the case of this volume there is a special measure of thanks that is necessary. I made the foolish mistake of writing the first six chapters on a hard-disc word processor without putting them on backup floppy discs. In the middle of my work my computer broke, and it was apparent that I had lost the chapters completely. We sent the machine to several repair shops over a course of weeks, only to be told that nothing could be done to retrieve the work. Then Chuck Swindoll heard of my plight and urged me to send the broken computer to his son, whom Chuck described as a "computer whiz." Within a few days, Curt Swindoll retrieved my material and solved my problem. To him goes my profound thanks and appreciation. I also want to thank Dr. Wendell Hawley of Tyndale House; my wife, Vesta; my administrative assistant, Maureen Buchman; and Ligonier's director of data processing, Gwen Weber, for all their help in the preparation of the manuscript. Special thanks also to Stephen Lang for his kind and gentle editorial help and the improvements he brought to this work.

Orlando, March 1990

CHAPTER ONE

GLORY IN THE FIELDS

While shepherds watched
their flocks by night
All seated on the ground,
The angel of the Lord came down,
And glory shone around.

NAHUM TATE

THERE IS SOMETHING almost mystical about Palestine. It is the Holy Land, the focal point of the pilgrim's quest for sacred time and space. A journey there is like traveling through a time warp.

Visiting the Holy Land involves more than culture shock. There is the added shock to the soul that comes from entering the arena of the incarnation. History becomes almost tactile. The flesh tingles at the sensation of suspended time. It's in the air. It's etched upon the barren rocks. The landscape, the vista, the roads, the Bedouin nomads, the undersized donkeys—they all say that this is where the Lord of the cosmos visited us.

There is a vast difference between the *historical* and the *historic*. Everything that happens in time and space is historical. But only the significant is historic. The *significant* is so-called because of its "sign" character. Something that is significant points beyond itself to something greater. No land is more packed with the historic and the significant than Palestine. Here the events that define all history took place. The very meaning of my life, the very roots of my existence are embedded in the stones of this land.

There are words in Luke's account of the nativity of Jesus that burn in my heart every time I hear them. They are the words shepherds spoke to each other after being visited by an angelic host: "Let's go to Bethlehem and see this thing that has happened, which the Lord has told us about." I went to Bethlehem as part of my pilgrimage to Israel. Bethlehem is a small town about five miles southwest of Jerusalem. The village had a rich history even before the birth of Jesus. The tomb of Rachel was in this locale (Genesis 35:19). It was the setting for much of the Old Testament Book of Ruth. The most famous Old Testament citizen of Bethlehem was David. Here he was anointed by Samuel. It was of this town that the prophet Micah wrote:

But you, Bethlehem Ephrathah,
*   though you are small among the clans of Judah,*
out of you will come for me
*   one who will be ruler over Israel,*
whose origins are from of old,
*   from ancient times.*

(Micah 5:2)

My visit to Bethlehem followed the normal pattern of tourists. We went by bus to the traditional site of the birth of Jesus. The site is marked by the Church of the Nativity, originally built by Byzantine emperor Justinian I in the sixth century. There we found the grotto of the nativity carved out of rock and lined with marble in a cave beneath a crypt.

The splendor of this church stands in marked contrast to the crudeness of the original manger scene. The biblical record of Jesus' birth places a strong accent on the humble accommodations made necessary because of the lack of room in the inn.

Each year during the Christmas season we hear about the lowly aspects of Jesus' birth. We hear of swaddling

14

clothes, a manger, the arduous journey of a peasant woman and her husband. These humble realities underscore the humiliation that marked the entrance of Christ into the world.

With these aspects of the birth of Jesus we are made aware of His willingness to empty Himself of the glory He enjoyed with the Father from all eternity. His lowly entrance into the world involved a veil that concealed His eternal majesty. It was His willingness to subject Himself to this humiliation that provoked Paul's hymn of Philippians 2:

Your attitude should be the same as that of Christ Jesus: Who, being in very nature God, did not consider equality with God something to be grasped, but made himself nothing, taking the very nature of a servant, being made in human likeness. And being found in appearance as a man, he humbled himself and became obedient to death—even death on a cross! Therefore God exalted him to the highest place and gave him the name that is above every name, that at the name of Jesus every knee should bow, in heaven and on earth and under the earth, and every tongue confess that Jesus Christ is Lord, to the glory of God the Father. (Philippians 2:5-11)

This hymn celebrates the honor of Christ that is restored to Him after His earthly humiliation. It reflects both upon His descending from heaven and His subsequent ascending to heaven. Before He could ascend to glory He had to first descend from glory.

In 1969 I met an elderly gentleman, Henry Barraclough. He had written a hymn that became famous— "Ivory Palaces." He told me that when he was a young man living in Philadelphia he heard a stirring sermon based on Paul's hymn in Philippians 2. After the sermon, Henry sat down and wrote the words to the hymn: "Out of the ivory palaces, into a world of woe...." Jesus descended to a world of woe, with His divine glory hidden beneath the veil of His humiliation. The veil was there, but it was not opaque. It allowed rays of light to shine through from time to time. In His most inglorious moments, in moments of radical passion and debasement, there are glimpses of the radiance that belonged to His divine nature.

Even in the humble circumstances of His birth there was a breakthrough of glory. It occurred in the fields outside Bethlehem. During my visit to Bethlehem I was listening to the tour guide's speech inside the Church of the Nativity when I felt drawn to leave the building and go outside. I wandered away from the tour group and walked to an old stone wall that marked the border to the fields of Bethlehem. I sat on the edge of the wall and gazed out over the vast expanse of empty fields. I closed my eyes and imagined that it was night—*that* night, the night the shepherds were keeping watch over their flocks. I thought about what it must be like to have a job that requires vigilance twenty-four hours a day. I remembered working night shifts in a factory and feeling the tedium that goes with the late hours.

Monotony goes with a job that follows the same routine day after day. The shepherds had spent countless nights in the fields outside Bethlehem. There would normally be little excitement.

16

But on the night Jesus was born something spectacular took place. The plains of Bethlehem became the theater for one of the most spectacular sound-and-light shows in human history. All heaven broke loose.

Luke tells us what happened:

And there were shepherds living out in the fields nearby, keeping watch over their flocks at night. An angel of the Lord appeared to them, and the glory of the Lord shone around them, and they were terrified. But the angel said to them, "Do not be afraid. I bring you good news of great joy that will be for all the people. Today in the town of David a Savior has been born to you; he is Christ the Lord. This will be a sign to you: You will find a baby wrapped in cloths and lying in a manger."

Suddenly a great company of the heavenly host appeared with the angel, praising God and saying,

"Glory to God in the highest, and on earth peace to men on whom his favor rests." (Luke 2:8-14)

The angelic visitor was surrounded by the glory of God. The glory was shining. This glory did not belong to the angel himself. It was God's glory, signifying His divine mode of being. It was the divine splendor that shrouded the heavenly messenger, a visible divine radiance.

The basic meaning of the word *angel* is "messenger." The angel is a spirit being who serves in the presence of God and who may be dispatched as a herald or messenger. He is a bearer of a divine announcement. His credential is seen visibly by the accompaniment of the shining glory of God.

In Luke's record the immediate response of the

shepherds to this intrusion is stark terror. The older translators rendered the text, "And they were sore afraid." As I sat on the wall by the edge of the fields of Bethlehem I thought of the terror the shepherds experienced. I tried to imagine my own terror if I encountered the same phenomenon. It would be like crossing a dimensional zone, staring at a vision few mortals have ever witnessed. I trembled even to think of it. I thought of the response of Habakkuk when God appeared to him: "When I heard, my body trembled; My lips quivered at the voice; Rottenness entered my bones; and I trembled in myself, that I might rest in the day of trouble" (Habakkuk 3:16, NKJV).

When the shepherds of Bethlehem quaked in fear, they were admonished by the angel: "Do not be afraid, for behold I bring you good tidings of great joy which will be to all people. For there is born to you this day in the city of David a Savior, who is Christ the Lord" (Luke 2:10-11, NKJV).

Every human being longs for a savior of some type. We look for someone or something that will solve our problems, ease our pain, or grant the most elusive goal of all, happiness. From the pursuit of success in business to the discovery of a perfect mate or friend, we make our search.

Even in the preoccupation with sports we show a hope for a savior. As a sports season ends with far more losers than winners, we hear the cry from cities across the land—"Wait till next year!" Then comes the draft or a new crop of rookies, and the fans pin their hopes and dreams on the new kid who will bring glory to the team. The rookie, the new client, the new machine, the news that will arrive in tomorrow's mail—all are invested with more hope than any creature can possibly deliver.

The burst of light that flooded the fields of Bethlehem announced the advent of a Savior who was able to do the task.

We note that the newborn Savior is also called "Christ the Lord." To the astonished shepherds these titles were pregnant with meaning. This Savior is the Christ, the long-awaited Messiah of Israel. Every Jew remembered the promise of God that someday the Messiah, the Lord's anointed, would come to deliver Israel. This Messiah-Savior is also Lord. He not only will save His people but He will be their King, their Sovereign.

The angel declares that this Savior-Messiah-Lord is born "unto you." The divine announcement is not an oracle of judgment but the declaration of a gift. The newborn King is born *for us*.

Next the angel announced the giving of a sign that would verify the truth of the declaration: "And this will be the sign to you: You will find a Babe wrapped in swaddling clothes, lying in a manger" (Luke 2:12, NKJV). The sign of the manger child contrasts with the explosion of glory in the field. Just a short distance away from the scene of light and sound will be found the Savior cloaked in humility and lowliness.

When the ethereal chorus was finished, the shepherds discussed the matter among themselves. One wonders about the tempo of the discussion. It could hardly have been calm. The men were obviously beside themselves with fear, excitement, awe, and delirious joy. They decided to leave at once for the promised sign.

The Scriptures tell us that they left with haste to search for the birthplace of the Christ. Again we wonder if in their haste and excitement they left their flocks unattended. Such an action would be unthinkable for any responsible shepherd. Did they leave one or more of their comrades behind? If so, how would those left behind feel about missing this adventure of all adventures? The Bible is silent on these questions and we are left with mere speculation about them.

Luke concludes the narrative of the shepherds by writing:

So they hurried off and found Mary and Joseph, and the baby, who was lying in the manger. When they had seen him, they spread the word concerning what had been told them about this child, and all who heard it were amazed at what the shepherds said to them. But Mary treasured up all these things and pondered them in her heart. The shepherds returned, glorifying and praising God for all the things they had heard and seen, which were just as they had been told. (Luke 2:16-20)

The shepherds went back to their flocks. The return trip was marked by unbridled adoration and praise. These men would never be the same. They had seen with their eyes and heard with their ears the manifestation of the glory of God.

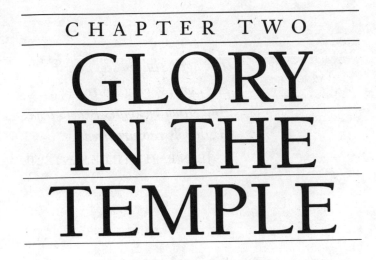

CHAPTER TWO

GLORY IN THE TEMPLE

The aged Simeon sees at last
His Lord, so long desired.
And Anna welcomes Israel's hope
With holy rapture fired.
JEAN BAPTISTE DE SANTEUIL

EIGHT DAYS after the wondrous birth of Jesus His parents had Him circumcised according to the regulations established in Jewish law. This was done in accord with the Law of Moses in the Old Testament:

The LORD said to Moses, "Say to the Israelites: 'A woman who becomes pregnant and gives birth to a son will be ceremonially unclean for seven days, just as she is unclean during her monthly period. On the eighth day the boy is to be circumcised. Then the woman must wait thirty-three days to be purified from her bleeding. She must not touch anything sacred or go to the sanctuary until the days of her purification are over. If she gives birth to a daughter, for two weeks the woman will be unclean, as during her period. Then she must wait sixty-six days to be purified from her bleeding.

" 'When the days of her purification for a son or daughter are over, she is to bring to the priest at the entrance to the Tent of Meeting a year-old lamb for a burnt offering and a young pigeon or a dove for a sin offering. He shall offer them before the LORD to make atonement for her, and then she will be ceremonially clean from her flow of blood. These are the regulations for the woman who gives birth to a boy or a girl.

" 'If she cannot afford a lamb, she is to bring two doves or two young pigeons, one for a burnt offering and the other for a sin offering. In this way the priest will make atonement for her, and she will be clean.' " (Leviticus 12:1-8)

The rite of circumcision had been instituted by God as an outward sign of His covenant with Abraham. The word *covenant* indicates an agreement or contract between two or more parties. The ancient Jewish covenant followed a format that was common in the Near East.

Modern research has uncovered interesting parallels between covenants found in the Bible and those found among the Hittite kings. The Hittite covenants were called "suzerain treaties." They involved contracts between the king (the suzerain) and his vassals. These treaties followed a regular form or pattern. The elements of the treaty included the following items:

1. Preamble
2. Historical prologue
3. Stipulations
4. Oaths
5. Sanctions
6. Rites of ratification
7. Provisions for public reading

The preamble of the covenant identified the name of the king, who was the sovereign or lord of the covenant. The historical prologue rehearsed the history of the relationship between the king and his vassals. (At times of covenant renewal, the prologue was brought up to date.)

In the case of the covenant God made with Moses at Mount Sinai we see the preamble and the historical prologue in these words: "And God spoke all these words: 'I am the LORD your God, who brought you out of Egypt, out of the land of slavery'" (Exodus 20:1). Here God identifies Himself by His name and by His historical involvement in the life of His people. He is the God who brought His people out of slavery.

Following this introduction, God delivered the Ten Commandments to Moses. The Ten Commandments, or Decalogue, were the stipulations of the covenant. The stipulations were the terms, the obligations, of the agreement.

After the stipulations were set forth, the sanctions of the covenant were declared. The sanctions were of two sorts. They included a promise of reward for those who obeyed the terms of the covenant and a threat of punishment if the terms of the contract were violated. In the framework of Old Testament covenants the sanctions were expressed in terms of blessings and curses. We see this in the Book of Deuteronomy:

See, I am setting before you today a blessing and a curse—the blessing if you obey the commands of the LORD your God that I am giving you today; the curse if you disobey the commands of the LORD your God and turn from the way that I command you today by following other gods, which you have not known. (Deuteronomy 11:26-28)

Once the terms of the covenant were agreed upon, the members of the covenant swore an oath to uphold it. God Himself, as the Sovereign of the covenant, swore to uphold His part of the agreement. The Letter to the Hebrews reminds us of the divine pledge:

When God made his promise to Abraham, since there was no one greater for him to swear by, he swore by himself, saying, "I will surely bless you and give you many descendants." And so after waiting patiently, Abraham received what was promised.

Men swear by someone greater than themselves, and the

25

oath confirms what is said and puts an end to all argument. Because God wanted to make the unchanging nature of his purpose very clear to the heirs of what was promised, he confirmed it with an oath. God did this so that, by two unchangeable things in which it is impossible for God to lie, we who have fled to take hold of the hope offered to us may be greatly encouraged. We have this hope as an anchor for the soul, firm and secure. It enters the inner sanctuary behind the curtain, where Jesus, who went before us, has entered on our behalf. He has become a high priest forever, in the order of Melchizedek. (Hebrews 6:13-20)

A vital part of the covenant was its ratification. The ratification usually involved a rite of blood. The Hebrew word for "covenant" is *berith*. This term originally meant a "cutting." This is important because in ancient Israel a covenant treaty was not merely written but was cut in blood. The covenant with Moses was ratified in blood:

Moses took half of the blood and put it in bowls, and the other half he sprinkled on the altar. Then he took the Book of the Covenant and read it to the people. They responded, "We will do everything the LORD has said; we will obey."

Moses then took the blood, sprinkled it on the people and said, "This is the blood of the covenant that the LORD has made with you in accordance with all these words." (Exodus 24:6-8)

The original cutting rite that ratified God's covenant with Abraham was the cutting rite of circumcision:

Then God said to Abraham, "As for you, you must keep my covenant, you and your descendants after you for the generations to come. This is my covenant with you and your descendants after you, the covenant you are to keep:

Every male among you shall be circumcised. You are to undergo circumcision, and it will be the sign of the covenant between me and you. For the generations to come every male among you who is eight days old must be circumcised, including those born in your household or bought with money from a foreigner—those who are not your offspring. Whether born in your household or bought with your money, they must be circumcised. My covenant in your flesh is to be an everlasting covenant. Any uncircumcised male, who has not been circumcised in the flesh, will be cut off from his people; he has broken my covenant." (Genesis 17:9-14)

The dual sanctions of the covenant are signified in the cutting rite of circumcision. Circumcision is both the sign of the blessing and of the curse. It signifies the promise of blessing in that as the foreskin is cut off or separated from the body, so Israel is separated out from or consecrated to the Lord. The descendants of Abraham are promised a special blessing if they keep faith with the covenant. The special privileges or blessings are marked in the flesh of those circumcised. At the same time the circumcised flesh is a perpetual reminder of the curse that will fall upon those who disobey the stipulations. The penalty for failure to circumcise the male child was to be "cut off from his people." One was either circumcised unto God or circumcised apart from God and the nation.

As a sign of the curse of the covenant, circumcision symbolized this idea: "If I fail to keep the terms of the covenant I will be cut off from God and all His benefits even as the foreskin of my flesh has been cut off."

The dramatic symbolism of this rite finds its highest

27

expression in the crucifixion of Christ. When Jesus dies on the cross, He takes upon Himself the full curse due to His people. The cross is the ultimate rite of circumcision. Paul sets this forth in the New Testament:

Christ redeemed us from the curse of the law by becoming a curse for us, for it is written: "Cursed is everyone who is hung on a tree." He redeemed us in order that the blessing given to Abraham might come to the Gentiles through Christ Jesus, so that by faith we might receive the promise of the Spirit. (Galatians 3:13-14)

When Jesus is presented by His parents for circumcision, we see His submission to the Law of the covenant. Jesus now becomes an heir to the covenant of Israel. That the sanctions of the covenant are imposed upon the Son of God indicates both His humiliation and His glory. He now enters His role as the New Adam, the author of a glorified humanity. He is the One destined to fulfill the Law in every detail and to win the blessings of the covenant for His people. Where we fail and become covenant-breakers, deserving the curse of the covenant, Jesus, our champion, succeeds in His role as the New Adam, the supreme covenant-keeper.

We are not merely redeemed by the death of Christ; we are also redeemed by the life of Christ. His death on the cross reveals the nadir of His humiliation as He bears the curse for us. But that is only part of His redemptive achievement. It is not enough for us merely to have our sins atoned for. To receive the blessings of the covenant we must possess real righteousness. We need what we cannot supply for ourselves. This merit of righteousness is earned for us by Jesus' life of perfect obedience.

We see then that by undergoing circumcision Jesus is not merely part of a meaningless ritual; He is embarking on a course of redemption as the New Adam.

At the time Jesus is presented for circumcision He also receives His name: "On the eighth day, when it was time to circumcise him, he was named Jesus, the name the angel had given him before he had been conceived" (Luke 2:21).

Jesus did not receive His name from Mary and Joseph. It was customary for the parents of a child to bestow the child's name upon him. But in the case of Jesus, His name was mandated by the angel:

But after he had considered this, an angel of the Lord appeared to him in a dream and said, "Joseph son of David, do not be afraid to take Mary home as your wife, because what is conceived in her is from the Holy Spirit. She will give birth to a son, and you are to give him the name Jesus, because he will save his people from their sins." (Matthew 1:20-21)

Adam and Eve were given dominion over the earth. One important dimension of that was the task of naming the animals. By giving the animals their names, Adam exercised His authority over them. When Jacob wrestled with the angel, the angel demanded Jacob to reveal his name. When Jacob uttered his own name, it was a sign of submission to the angel. Then the angel changed Jacob's name from Jacob to Israel (see Genesis 33:24-28).

In the case of Jesus the selection of His name is not left to His earthly parents. God reserves the right to name Jesus. God does this in cases of those chosen for a particular holy vocation, as with John the Baptist.

The reason given by the angel for the name of Jesus is twofold. In the first instance it is because of the unique circumstances of Jesus' conception and birth. Jesus is uniquely the Son of God. He is the *monogene*, the "only begotten" of the Father (John 1:14). His conception differs from that of any other child. He is conceived, not by the ordinary means of human generation, but by the power of the Holy Spirit:

"How will this be," Mary asked the angel, "since I am a virgin?" The angel answered, "The Holy Spirit will come upon you, and the power of the Most High will overshadow you. So the holy one to be born will be called the Son of God." (Luke 1:34-35)

The conception of Jesus calls attention to the glory that surrounds His birth. The virgin birth is not explained in detail by the New Testament. We are told simply that the Holy Spirit would come upon Mary and "overshadow" her. This overshadowing is not elucidated in terms of biology. It is reminiscent, however, of the divine power and method of creation itself. The act of divine creation demonstrates the power to bring something out of nothing. The conception of a baby in the womb of Mary is a divine act of creation *ex nihilo*, out of nothing. It is a work that only God can perform. The normal process of union of sperm and ovum is bypassed. This child is conceived by the power of the Holy Spirit.

We are reminded here of the Genesis account of

Creation. We read in the biblical narrative this description of the original Creation: "Now the earth was formless and empty, darkness was over the surface of the deep, and the Spirit of God was hovering over the waters" (Genesis 1:2). The hovering of the Spirit over the deep was the pulsating beginning of the universe. As the Holy Spirit overshadowed the deep and brought forth a created universe, so the same Spirit overshadowed a peasant virgin to conceive the Son of God.

The second significance of the naming of Jesus goes beyond the matter of the source of His life and touches upon the purpose of it. His name is given by God to indicate His divine vocation. He is called "Jesus"—the name means "God saves"—because His task is to save His people from their sin.

Though Jesus' birth was attended by humiliation, especially in His subjection to the stipulations of the covenant and His exposure to the curse of the Law, His birth was not without elements of glory. His conception was in glory and His vocation indicated by His name was a glorious vocation.

The Bible gives us sparse information about the childhood of Jesus. We have information regarding His birth, His circumcision, His dedication in the temple, and His visit to Jerusalem at the age of twelve. What happened to Jesus between the first few weeks of His life and age twelve, and between age twelve and the beginning of His public ministry at about age thirty, is virtually unknown.

This gap in the biographical data of the life of Christ

is both astonishing and disconcerting. It is astonishing in that Jesus is clearly the most famous and most studied personage from the ancient world. Yet we know next to nothing of the vast majority of the years of His life. The Synoptic Gospels (Matthew, Mark, and Luke) give us a sketchy biography with a heavy concentration on the last three years of His life. John's Gospel spends about two-thirds of its pages on the last week of Jesus' life.

Apart from the biblical record of the life of Jesus we have little information from His contemporaries. From historians such as Josephus and Suetonius we have information that totals about three paragraphs. (This dearth of information has led some skeptics to raise questions of whether Jesus even existed.) We must content ourselves with what we find in the Bible.

One interesting footnote to the information gap of the early life of Jesus is found in the so-called Apocryphal Gospels that were written after the New Testament. These are fraudulent accounts of Jesus' life, written mostly by heretics as part of their propaganda. Here the missing years of Jesus' life are filled in with fanciful accounts of His youth. This literature portrays a child who uses His miraculous powers in frivolous and irresponsible ways. When left to play in solitude, Jesus fashions playmates for Himself by molding birds from clay and then turning them into living creatures. The portrait here is of a childish magician who uses His supernatural power for sheer self-indulgence.

Though the biblical record of Jesus' youth is sparse,

it is nevertheless significant. Luke gives us information regarding the events that followed shortly upon His circumcision:

When the time of their purification according to the Law of Moses had been completed, Joseph and Mary took him to Jerusalem to present him to the Lord (as it is written in the Law of the Lord, "Every firstborn male is to be consecrated to the Lord"), and to offer a sacrifice in keeping with what is said in the Law of the Lord: "a pair of doves or two young pigeons." (Luke 2:22-24)

When Jesus' parents took Him to Jerusalem to dedicate Him to the Lord, the sacrifice they offered was a pair of doves and two young pigeons. This rite fulfilled the law that made a special provision for purification of poverty-stricken parents. The usual offering was a lamb. But if the couple could not afford one, they could substitute turtledoves or pigeons: "If she cannot afford a lamb, she is to bring two doves or two young pigeons, one for a burnt offering and the other for a sin offering. In this way the priest will make atonement for her, and she will be clean" (Leviticus 12:8). That Joseph and Mary offered the substitute sacrifice speaks of the cloak of humility that Jesus wore. It would not have been construed by contemporaries as a manifestation of regal glory. Yet the circumstances that prevailed in the drama of the purification rite lend another dimension to the account. At the dedication in the temple, Jesus and His parents were met by two remarkable persons, Simeon and Anna, whose responses to the Christ child gave more than tiny hints of His glory:

Now there was a man in Jerusalem called Simeon, who was righteous and devout. He was waiting for the consolation of Israel, and the Holy Spirit was upon him. It had been revealed to him by the Holy Spirit that he would not die before he had seen the Lord's Christ. Moved by the Spirit, he went into the temple courts. When the parents brought in the child Jesus to do for him what the custom of the Law required, Simeon took him in his arms and praised God, saying:

"Sovereign Lord, as you have promised, you now dismiss your servant in peace.

For my eyes have seen your salvation, which you have prepared in the sight of all people,

a light for revelation to the Gentiles and for glory to your people Israel." (Luke 2:25-32)

Simeon is one of my favorite biblical characters. Though this brief passage gives us all we know of the man, we see in him one who is a model of biblical virtue. We see a man whose character was marked by steadfast faith and perseverance, virtues that receive the highest acclaim in the Word of God.

Simeon lived in a period of Jewish history that was marked by silence from heaven. From the closing of the Old Testament with the Book of Malachi to the birth of Jesus, four hundred years had elapsed. Four centuries had come and gone with no revelation from God. If we turned our own calendar back four hundred years, we would reach the closing years of the sixteenth century. The Protestant Reformation was still in its embryonic stages. The Pilgrims had not yet sailed for the New World. History knew nothing of philosophers Descartes, Hume, or Kant. There had been no Napoleon, no

George Washington, no Karl Marx. There was no French Revolution, American Revolution, or Industrial Revolution. There were no electric lights, automobiles, airplanes, or television. No one spoke of world wars. A lot of water goes under the bridge in four hundred years.

Because of the protracted silence from God, much of the zeal for religion had grown cold in Israel. People were more interested in the latest decrees from Rome than in ancient mandates given at Sinai.

Not so for Simeon. He is described as being just and devout. He was a righteous and godly man. He was a man-in-waiting. He patiently awaited what Luke calls the "Consolation of Israel." This was a technical term. It functioned as one of the many titles ascribed to the promised Messiah. One of the tasks the Messiah would perform was to bring comfort—consolation—to His people.

When Christians speak of the Comforter, or Paraclete, they usually have in mind the Holy Spirit. The Spirit is named by Jesus as Comforter or Paraclete:

"And I will ask the Father, and he will give you another Counselor to be with you forever—the Spirit of truth. The world cannot accept him, because it neither sees him nor knows him. But you know him, for he lives with you and will be in you." (John 14:16-17)

In the New International translation of the Bible, the title *Comforter* is rendered by the word *Counselor*. But this Counselor or Paraclete is described as "another" Counselor. He is the *second* Paraclete who comes to represent the presence of the original Comforter. Jesus

is the original Paraclete. John makes that clear elsewhere in his epistles:

*My dear children, I write this to you so that you will not
sin. But if anybody does sin, we have one who speaks to the
Father in our defense—Jesus Christ, the Righteous One.*
(1 John 2:1)

Jesus is identified as the original Comforter, the Consolation of Israel.

Simeon received a special revelation from God in
which he was told he would not die until he saw the
Messiah. When he came to the temple on the day Mary
and Joseph arrived with the infant Jesus, Simeon sang the
song often known by its first Latin words, *Nunc Dimittis:*
"Lord, now you are letting Your servant depart in peace,
according to Your word; for my eyes have seen your
salvation." For Simeon this was not a moment of resig-
nation to the dreadful tragedy of death. On the contrary,
it was a moment of supreme glory. His eyes had just
beheld the fulfillment of the promise of God for the thing
his soul longed for the most. Simeon's song was a celebration of unspeakable joy. It was the song of a man who
had just experienced the fullest measure of contentment
possible to mortal man. He had seen Christ. He did not
need to witness the earthly ministry of the adult Jesus. He
did not need to see the crucifixion or the Resurrection.
He saw the Incarnate God, breathing and present in His
mother's arms. That was enough. Simeon was ready to
die a contented man. Simeon beheld the light that would
bring salvation to the Gentiles and was "the glory of Your
people Israel." Mary and Joseph's response to the words

of Simeon was one of amazement: "The child's father and mother marveled at what was said about him" (Luke 2:33). As the parents of Jesus stood marveling, Simeon spoke again:

"This child is destined to cause the falling and rising of many in Israel, and to be a sign that will be spoken against, so that the thoughts of many hearts will be revealed. And a sword will pierce your own soul too."
(Luke 2:34-35)

Simeon's words were a sort of prophecy. They contained both words of triumph and words that carried an ominous warning. One wonders if Mary later recalled these words when she stood at the foot of the cross watching her son be executed. I wonder if, when the centurion thrust his spear into the side of Jesus, Mary sensed a sword piercing her own soul.

Simeon was not the only person Mary and Joseph encountered in the temple. Luke also mentions the prophetess Anna:

There was also a prophetess, Anna, the daughter of Phanuel, of the tribe of Asher. She was very old; she had lived with her husband seven years after her marriage, and then was a widow until she was eighty-four. She never left the temple but worshiped night and day, fasting and praying. Coming up to them at that very moment, she gave thanks to God and spoke about the child to all who were looking forward to the redemption of Jerusalem.
(Luke 2:36-38)

Like Simeon the venerable Anna had spent decades in righteous devotion to God. She took up residence in the temple, devoting herself to prayer and fasting. Like

Simeon, she saw with her own eyes the fruit of her years of praying and fasting. Under the Spirit she expressed praise and thanksgiving for the infant who was now present.

A crucial aspect of Jesus' humiliation was the hiddenness of His glory. His identity was often concealed. We hear the protests from the wounded egos of famous people when they are not recognized. They complain, "Don't you know who I am?" It is humiliating to them to go unrecognized. Because people do not recognize them, they feel treated beneath their dignity. If any human being was ever subjected to such repeated indignities during His life, it was Jesus. During His earthly ministry the ones who most often and most clearly recognized Him were the demons from hell.

But in this episode the identity of Jesus does not go unrecognized. Simeon and Anna see the glory of Christ.

After Mary and Joseph completed their visit to the temple in Jerusalem, they returned to Nazareth in Galilee. The only mention we have of events after that are in Matthew's account of the flight into Egypt and Luke's terse statement of Jesus' continued growth. Matthew records these words:

When they had gone, an angel of the Lord appeared to Joseph in a dream. "Get up," he said, "take the child and his mother and escape to Egypt. Stay there until I tell you, for Herod is going to search for the child to kill him."

So he got up, took the child and his mother during the night and left for Egypt, where he stayed until the death of Herod. And so was fulfilled what the Lord had said through the prophet: "Out of Egypt I called my son."

When Herod realized that he had been outwitted by the Magi, he was furious, and he gave orders to kill all the boys in Bethlehem and its vicinity who were two years old and under, in accordance with the time he had learned from the Magi. Then what was said through the prophet Jeremiah was fulfilled:

"A voice is heard in Ramah, weeping and great mourning,

Rachel weeping for her children and refusing to be comforted,

because they are no more."

After Herod died, an angel of the Lord appeared in a dream to Joseph in Egypt and said, "Get up, take the child and his mother and go to the land of Israel, for those who were trying to take the child's life are dead."

So he got up, took the child and his mother and went to the land of Israel. But when he heard that Archelaus was reigning in Judea in place of his father Herod, he was afraid to go there. Having been warned in a dream, he withdrew to the district of Galilee, and he went and lived in a town called Nazareth. So was fulfilled what was said through the prophets: "He will be called a Nazarene." (Matthew 2:13-23)

Luke adds to this sketchy outline these words: "And the child grew and became strong; he was filled with wisdom, and the grace of God was upon him" (Luke 2:40). His brief summary of the developmental years of Jesus life tells us that Jesus went though a period of both physical and spiritual growth. It was a growth marked by the presence of the grace of God. An amplification of this is added by the author of Hebrews:

Although he was a son, he learned obedience from what he suffered and, once made perfect, he became the source of

*eternal salvation for all who obey him and was designated
by God to be high priest in the order of Melchizedek.*
(Hebrews 5:8)

Here the text speaks of learning "obedience" and of
being made "perfect." This raises the question of
whether Jesus had to grow from disobedience to obedience or from imperfection to perfection. The question
is intensified by the other incident noted in Scripture
about Jesus' visit to Jerusalem the age of twelve. We will
examine these questions in the next chapter.

CHAPTER THREE

GLORY IN HIS CHILDHOOD

When Jesus left his Father's throne,
He chose a humble birth;
Like us, unhonored and unknown,
He came to dwell on earth.
Like him may we be found below
In wisdom's path of peace;
Like him in grace and knowledge grow
As years and strength increase.

JAMES MONTGOMERY

A NOTEWORTHY INCIDENT occurred in the childhood of Jesus during His visit to Jerusalem at age twelve. At age thirteen a Jewish boy became a man and went though the rite of bar mitzvah. It was customary for Jewish parents to take their sons to Jerusalem one year before bar mitzvah to acquaint them with the temple customs in preparation for the following year. It was a kind of dry run to familiarize them with temple procedures.

It was also customary for the family to make an annual pilgrimage to Jerusalem for the Passover. The families and friends from various outlying towns would make the journey by caravan. It was a gala occasion as well as a solemn religious event. Luke gives this account:

Every year his parents went to Jerusalem for the Feast of the Passover. When he was twelve years old, they went up to the Feast, according to the custom. After the Feast was over, while his parents were returning home, the boy Jesus stayed behind in Jerusalem, but they were unaware of it. Thinking he was in their company, they traveled on for a day. Then they began looking for him among their relatives and friends. When they did not find him, they went back to Jerusalem to look for him. After three days they found him in the temple courts, sitting among the teachers, listening to them and asking them questions. Everyone who heard him was amazed at his understanding and his answers. When his parents saw him, they were astonished. His mother said to him, "Son, why have you treated us like this? Your father and I have been anxiously searching for you."

"Why were you searching for me?" he asked. "Didn't you know I had to be in my Father's house?" But they did not understand what he was saying to them. (Luke 2:41-50)

Mary and Joseph experienced a frightening episode, one that strikes terror in the hearts of parents. After the feast had ended and the families packed their belongings for the journey home, Jesus' parents discovered that their son was not with the company. They had already traveled a day's journey before they realized He was missing. They searched the other groups to see if He was traveling with friends or relatives, but Jesus could not be found. He had stayed behind in Jerusalem and obviously not told His parents that He was lingering.

My wife and I laugh at our remembrance of an episode that occurred when our son was four. Vesta and I had driven to church in separate cars. She went early to sing in the choir. After church I drove home assuming that she had our son with her. She drove home assuming that I had him with me. When we met at the house, we were horrified to discover our error. We hastened back to the church, where we found our son playing, oblivious to his recent abandonment. We hugged him with joy as we expressed our relief to find him. But this oversight was one that was rectified in a few minutes. I cannot imagine what we would have felt had we not discovered our error for twenty-four hours.

In the light of what the Scriptures teach concerning

the sinless humanity of Jesus, the failure of His parents in this instance is understandable. They were rearing a perfect child. They were obviously not accustomed to their son not being where He was supposed to be at any given time. Also, given the closeness of extended families in those days, the parents would have assumed that the child was with other family members.

When Mary and Joseph discovered that Jesus was missing, they hurried back to Jerusalem to look for Him. The Bible does not tell how long the return trip took. It might have taken a day's journey for them to get back to the city. If so, this would mean that they would now have been separated from their son for at least two days. Luke reports that it was "after three days they found him in the temple." The text is unclear about the exact reference of this three days. Was it three days after they left Jerusalem? Or was it three days after their return to Jerusalem? If it means the latter, that would then mean that they were separated from their son for a period of five days. Mary must have been beside herself with anxiety, and Joseph no less worried. Luke tells us of the scene of Mary and Joseph finding their lost son:

After three days they found him in the temple courts, sitting among the teachers, listening to them and asking them questions. Everyone who heard him was amazed at his understanding and his answers. (Luke 2:46-47)

We see here an almost humorous exercise in contrasts. While Mary and Joseph were frantic, Jesus appears relaxed in the company of the teachers of the Law. Here is Jesus, a twelve-year-old boy, having a discussion with learned theologians. There have been occasions in history when adults have been amazed by the feats of child prodigies. Mozart as a child amazed his contemporaries with his musical ability. Yet the world never before had met a prodigy to compare with the twelve-year-old Jesus.

I am a theologian by training, vocation, and profession. When my own son was twelve, he was studying Latin and French and reading the likes of Huxley. He asked me many penetrating theological questions then. Now he is twenty-four and a student in the seminary where I teach. He sits in my classroom taking copious notes. Then at home he grills me with his questions. He can be tough. More than once he has made me uncomfortable. But he has never yet (with the emphasis on the yet) intimidated me.

But imagine having a theological discussion with the Son of God. I hope I would have the good sense to sit down and turn the blackboard over to Him. If Jesus showed up in my classroom, I would be the one taking the notes.

Of course, when Jesus was in the temple the teachers there did not know they were entertaining God incarnate. But they did realize that they were dealing with an extraordinarily gifted young man. Luke tells us that they "were astonished at His understanding and answers" (NKJV). What was the cause of their astonishment? It is the church's conviction that in Jesus we meet the One who is the God-man. That is, we confess that Jesus was *vere homo* (truly man) and *vere deus* (truly

God). Now we know that God is omniscient. He knows everything there is to know. We also know that Jesus had a divine nature. Does this mean that Jesus knew everything?

Touching His divine nature, Jesus was clearly omniscient. Touching His human nature, however, He was not. Jesus learned things. There were some things he declared He did not know. We see this clearly in Mark's Gospel: "No one knows about that day or hour, not even the angels in heaven, nor the Son, but only the Father" (Mark 13:32). It is both possible and necessary for us to distinguish between the divine and human natures of Christ. For example, when Jesus was hungry and when He sweated, these were manifestations of His human nature, not His divine nature. God does not eat. God does not sweat. However, though it is necessary to distinguish the two natures of Christ, it is equally necessary that we neither divide nor separate them.

Because the two natures of Christ reside in an indivisible unity, many theologians insist that the attribute of omniscience is communicated to the human nature from the divine nature. That is, whatever the divine nature knows, the human nature knows as well. The passage cited from Mark in which Jesus declared that there was at least one thing the Son did not know—the day and the hour of His *parousia* (coming)—is then explained by these theologians as involving some sort of accommodation of Jesus to His hearers. That is, Jesus really did know the day and the hour, but for some reason He was unwilling or unable to reveal it at that time. Perhaps the knowledge was too high or to holy to be uttered. So He accommodated them by telling them He didn't know. This explanation, as forced as it appears to be, does much to preserve the omniscience of Jesus. But it does so at a severe cost. This explanation raises more problems than it solves precisely because it casts a heavy shadow upon Jesus' integrity. It leaves us with Jesus saying that He does not know something that in fact He did know. The agony of such a desperate interpretation of Scripture is driven by the theologians' desire to insure that we maintain the unity of the two natures of Christ.

I do not think such interpretation of the text is necessary to preserve the unity of the two natures. There were times in His earthly ministry where Jesus displayed supernatural knowledge, a knowledge above and beyond what is accessible to human insight. (See His discussion with Nathanael in John 1.) Though the two natures of Jesus are united, they remain distinct from each other. They are as the Council of Chalcedon confessed in A.D. 451, without mixture, confusion, separation, and division, each nature retaining its own attributes.

In the union of the two natures there was also communion of the two natures. Obviously there was communion of information between the divine nature and the human nature. Because of the unity of the two natures, Jesus' human nature had access to the knowledge found in the divine omniscience. There could be a communication of knowledge between the divine and human natures

48

without a communion of attributes from the divine nature to the human nature. In the union of the divine and human natures, the divine nature remained divine and the human nature remained human.

Now it is possible that what astonished the teachers in the temple was a display of supernatural knowledge that the boy Jesus received from His divine nature. But it is not necessary to appeal to the divine in Jesus to account for His ability to astonish the learned professors. He could have done it with the sheer strength of His unaided perfect humanity.

When we think of Jesus' perfection, we tend to limit our thinking to His moral perfection. But there is far more to it than that. Jesus possessed a human nature that was unfallen. He, as the New Adam, must have had a nature like Adam's before the Fall.

The Fall of Adam has affected more than our behavior. The whole of our humanity has been ravaged by it. Our bodies have been ravaged. We suffer weaknesses and disease. None of our five senses escape the effects of sin. Most important, sin effects our minds. Theologians discuss what they call the *noetic* effects of sin. The word *noetic* has its roots in the Greek word for "mind" (*nous*).

Because of the effects of sin, no man thinks as clearly or as accurately as he would without the influence of sin. As the apostle Paul writes:

Although they knew God, they neither glorified him as God nor gave thanks to him, but their thinking became futile and their foolish hearts were darkened. Although they claimed to be wise, they became fools. (Romans 1:21-22)

Though our minds have been darkened, they have not been destroyed. We still have the capacity to think. Even a pagan can add two and two and get four. And we are still capable of learning. But what a fallen man can learn by age forty could easily be surpassed by what an unfallen person could learn by age twelve. A perfect twelve-year-old would be perfect in the clarity of his thought. His thinking would not be marred by errors of reasoning. The mind of the twelve-year-old Jesus would have been enough to astonish the most learned of fallen men.

But if Jesus was perfect, how can we account for His apparent disobedience or at least inconsideration for His parents shown in Luke's narrative?

When his parents saw him, they were astonished. His mother said to him, "Son, why have you treated us like this? Your father and I have been anxiously searching for you."

"Why were you searching for me?" he asked. "Didn't you know I had to be in my Father's house?" But they did not understand what he was saying to them. (Luke 2:48-50)

As relieved and amazed as Mary and Joseph were they were not without annoyance. All parents can easily identify with their ambivalent feelings. We worry about the safety of our children when they stay out too late, and when they return safely, we experience both relief and anger. When Jesus' parents confronted Him about His protracted and unexplained absence from them, Jesus responded with a question of His own that was a thinly veiled rebuke: "Why were you searching for me?

50

Did you not know I had to be in my Father's house?"
(Other translations read, "Did you not know that I had
to be about my Father's business?")

We must keep in mind a couple of crucial principles.
In the first place, Jesus was not only Mary and Joseph's
son, He was also Mary and Joseph's Lord. In one sense
Mary and Joseph's anxiety demonstrated unbelief in the
revealed nature of their son. If Mary pondered the
things that had already been revealed to her about her
son, she would have no reason to be distressed by the
episode. She should have known that her son and her
Lord was above acting in an irresponsible manner. The
Law of Moses required that every son must honor his
parents. Surely no son ever honored his parents more
than Jesus did. It was not a matter of His failure to
honor them but of their failure to honor Him. In a
deeper way, by not telling them of His intentions in the
temple and leaving them to their own implicit trust, He
showed high honor to His parents.

The second point of Jesus' reply focuses on His responsibility to obey His heavenly Father. Though every
human being is called to render obedience to earthly
authority, that obedience must be superseded by obedience to God. Jesus had a higher obligation to God than
He had to Mary and Joseph.

With His responding question, Jesus was reminding
His parents of His identity and His divine vocation. He
had a mission to perform that had been announced to
them by angels. Now that mission was beginning to be
realized.

Though this is the first mention of Scripture of Jesus rebuking His mother, it is not the last. He also found it necessary to rebuke her at the wedding feast of Cana (see John 2:3-5).

We conclude then that this narrative of Jesus amazing the teachers in the temple reveals the glory of His identity, of His mission, and most clearly, of His perfect human nature.

CHAPTER FOUR

GLORY BY THE RIVER

Manifest at Jordan's stream,
Prophet, Priest, and King supreme.
CHRISTOPHER WORDSWORTH

THE PUBLIC MINISTRY of Jesus begins with His baptism in the River Jordan at the hands of John the Baptist. John's work of baptism had created a public sensation and a furor among the clergy of his day. There was something radical about John that went well beyond his extraordinary dress style.

In those days John the Baptist came, preaching in the Desert of Judea and saying, "Repent, for the kingdom of heaven is near." This is he who was spoken of through the prophet Isaiah:
"A voice of one calling in the desert, 'Prepare the way for the Lord, make straight paths for him.'"
John's clothes were made of camel's hair, and he had a leather belt around his waist. His food was locusts and wild honey. People went out to him from Jerusalem and all Judea and the whole region of the Jordan. Confessing their sins, they were baptized by him in the Jordan River. (Matthew 3:1-6)

John's bizarre diet and clothing bespeak a man whose habitat was the desert. Remember that Israel had been without the voice of prophecy since the close of the Old Testament canon and the Book of Malachi. Now John appears on the scene coming out of the desert, the traditional meeting place between God and His prophets. John's style and his dress are reminiscent of the prophet Elijah.

That John conjured up memories of Elijah excited

interest concerning the possible fulfillment of the last prophecy of the Old Testament:

See, I will send you the prophet Elijah before that great and dreadful day of the LORD comes. He will turn the hearts of the fathers to their children, and the hearts of the children to their fathers; or else I will come and strike the land with a curse. (Malachi 4:5-6)

This final prophecy of the Old Testament linked the hope of the reappearance of Elijah as the signal for the coming of the long-awaited Messiah. Because of this expectation, the Jews sent a delegation to question John about his real identity:

Now this was John's testimony when the Jews of Jerusalem sent priests and Levites to ask him who he was. He did not fail to confess, but confessed freely, "I am not the Christ."
They asked him, "Then who are you? Are you Elijah?"
He said, "I am not."
"Are you the Prophet?"
He answered, "No."
Finally they said, "Who are you? Give us an answer to take back to those who sent us. What do you say about yourself?"
John replied in the words of Isaiah the prophet, "I am the voice of one calling in the desert, 'Make straight the way for the Lord.'" (John 1:19-23)

John clearly denies that he is Elijah. But the mystery surrounding the figure of John the Baptist deepens with Jesus' cryptic words about him:

As John's disciples were leaving, Jesus began to speak to the crowd about John: "What did you go out into the desert to see? A reed swayed by the wind? If not, what did you go out to see? A man dressed in fine clothes? No, those who wear fine clothes are in kings' palaces. Then what did you go out to see? A prophet? Yes, I tell you, and more than a prophet. This is the one about whom it is written:

> *'I will send my messenger ahead of you,*
> *who will prepare your way before you.'*

I tell you the truth: Among those born of women there has not risen anyone greater than John the Baptist; yet he who is least in the kingdom of heaven is greater than he. From the days of John the Baptist until now, the kingdom of heaven has been forcefully advancing, and forceful men lay hold of it. For all the Prophets and the Law prophesied until John. And if you are willing to accept it, he is the Elijah who was to come. He who has ears, let him hear.'" (Matthew 11:7-15)

Jesus makes two noteworthy statements about John here. First, He declares that "this is the one about whom it is written" and then proceeds to quote from Malachi's prophecy concerning the reappearance of Elijah. Second, Jesus declares, "If you are willing to accept it, he is the Elijah who was to come." The difficulty with this passage is obvious. Here Jesus declares that John the Baptist was Elijah. Yet when John was asked, "Are you Elijah?" he answered, "I am not." Was John the Baptist Elijah or not? John said no, Jesus said yes. However, when we look closely at the declaration of Jesus, we must see that His yes was a qualified yes. He prefaced His declaration with the words "if you are willing to receive it . . ." (Matthew 11:14). Then immediately following the declaration Jesus added the remark, "He who has ears to hear, let him hear!" (v. 15).

These qualifiers indicate that Jesus' identification of John with Elijah was meant to be understood in a special sense. John fulfilled the prophecy of the return of Elijah; he was not the actual reincarnation of Elijah himself. The difficulty is further resolved when the Scripture adds the additional explanation with the angel's announcement to the father of John:

But the angel said to him: "Do not be afraid, Zechariah; your prayer has been heard. Your wife Elizabeth will bear you a son, and you are to give him the name John. He will be a joy and delight to you, and many will rejoice because of his birth, for he will be great in the sight of the Lord. He is never to take wine or other fermented drink, and he will be filled with the Holy Spirit even from birth. Many of the people of Israel will he bring back to the Lord their God. And he will go on before the Lord, in the spirit and power of Elijah, to turn the hearts of the fathers to their children and the disobedient to the wisdom of the righteous—to make ready a people prepared for the Lord." (Luke 1:13-17)

Here the angel declares that John will come in the "spirit and power" of Elijah. John will represent the reinstitution of the role of the prophet. Indeed, he will occupy a position that no prophet before him enjoyed. The Old Testament prophets declared that sometime in the future the Messiah would come; John is the actual herald, or forerunner, of the Messiah. John stands on the threshold of the kingdom of God. He is the one who ushers in the King.

John's role as the herald of the King may be seen in the following Scriptures:

He went into all the country around the Jordan, preaching a baptism of repentance for the forgiveness of sins. As is written in the book of the words of Isaiah the prophet:

58

"A voice of one calling in the desert,
'Prepare the way for the Lord,
  make straight paths for him.
Every valley shall be filled in,
  every mountain and hill made low.
The crooked roads shall become straight,
  the rough ways smooth.
And all mankind will see God's salvation.'" (Luke 3:3-6)

"The ax is already at the root of the trees, and every tree
that does not produce good fruit will be cut down and
thrown into the fire." (Luke 3:9)

The people were waiting expectantly and were all
wondering in their hearts if John might possibly be the
Christ. John answered them all, "I baptize you with water.
But one more powerful than I will come, the thongs of
whose sandals I am not worthy to untie. He will baptize
you with the Holy Spirit and with fire. His winnowing
fork is in his hand to clear his threshing floor and to gather
the wheat into his barn, but he will burn up the chaff with
unquenchable fire." And with many other words John
exhorted the people and preached the good news to them.
(Luke 3:15-18)

John's preaching accented the radical nearness of the com-ing kingdom. He stressed that the kingdom of God was "at hand," at the point of breakthrough. John used two images to underscore the nearness of the kingdom. First he declared that "the ax is laid to the root of the trees." This was a symbol of imminent judgment. The coming of the Messiah would be a time of crisis for the people.

We notice that the image John used was that of the ax reaching the root or the core of the trees. He was not merely in the process of sharpening the ax. He had not merely begun to chip away at the outer bark of the trees. The ax had already penetrated to the core. The image suggests that one more strike from the ax will bring the tree crashing down.

The second image is also one of radical nearness. John speaks of the Messiah: "His winnowing fan is in his hand." This image suggests one of harvest and the separation of the wheat from the chaff. The winnowing fan functioned as a sort of pitchfork or rake. The farmer used the fan to reach into a pile of grain that contained both wheat and chaff. He would then fling the wheat and chaff together into the air. The wind would then do the work of separation. Since the chaff lacked the substance of the wheat, it was lighter, and the wind current would carry it away from the wheat.

Both images made one thing clear: The time of crisis had come. Repentance and baptism were essential.

John did not invent the ritual of baptism. There already was a rite of baptism well known to the Jews. It was called proselyte baptism.

This was a rite for Gentile converts to Judaism. Because Gentiles were considered "unclean," they had to undergo a purifying bath to be cleansed. This was the symbolic import of baptism that made John's ministry seem so outrageous to the Pharisees. John had come out of the desert and demanded that the Jews submit to baptism. In effect he was saying, "Your Messiah is about to come and you are not fit for His presence. You are unclean. You need to be purified."

John said to the crowds coming out to be baptized by him,
"You brood of vipers! Who warned you to flee from the
coming wrath? Produce fruit in keeping with repentance.
And do not begin to say to yourselves, 'We have Abraham
as our father.' For I tell you that out of these stones God
can raise up children for Abraham." (Luke 3:7-8)

So John's ministry of baptism was one of preparation
for the coming Messiah. When the Pharisees asked
John directly why he was baptizing, John explained:

They questioned him, "Why then do you baptize if you are
not the Christ, nor Elijah, nor the Prophet?"
"I baptize with water," John replied, "but among you
stands one you do not know. He is the one who comes after
me, the thongs of whose sandals I am not worthy to untie."
(John 1:25-27)

On the following day Jesus appeared on the shores of
the Jordan River. On this occasion John uttered the
Agnus Dei: "Behold! The Lamb of God who takes away
the sin of the world!"(John 1:29).

With this announcement the world gets a glimpse of
the glory of Christ. Here John declares that Jesus is the
promised Messiah. He is the Suffering Servant of Israel
prophesied by Isaiah.

What follows this announcement, however, is shocking.
Jesus, the one just identified as the sinless Lamb of God,
presents Himself for baptism. This hit John hard. Baptism was for repentance, for the cleansing of sin. How
could the Lamb of God submit Himself to it?

"John tried to deter him, saying, 'I need to be baptized
by you, and do you come to me?'" John had declared
Jesus' superiority to himself. John insists that he should

61

be baptized by Jesus, not the other way around. Jesus' reply to John is crucial for our understanding of the whole purpose of Jesus' baptism: "Jesus replied, 'Let it be so now; it is proper for us to do this to fulfill all righteousness.' Then John consented" (Matthew 3:15). Jesus' reply to John is prefaced with the words, "Let it be so now." Other renderings of the text include, "Suffer it now" or "Permit it to be so now." It is as if Jesus said, "Look, I don't have time to explain all this to you. Just indulge me for the moment. Trust me, I know what I am doing." The specific reason Jesus gives to John is this: "It is proper for us to do this to fulfill all righteousness."

This is the key to understanding Jesus' baptism. He submitted to baptism in order to fulfill all righteousness—that is, to do everything that God requires. Through the prophetic command of John the Baptist, God had added a new requirement to His covenant people, that they be cleansed in preparation for the coming of the kingdom. Whatever Israel was required to do, the Servant of Israel was required to fulfill for the nation. Jesus, as the Lamb of God, carries the entire burden of His people, including the requirement of baptism. For Jesus to become our righteousness, He had to fulfill every command of God.

Here at the Jordan we see His humiliation in His willingness to submit to baptism. Yet this act is not without a subsequent moment of glory.

As soon as Jesus was baptized, he went up out of the water. At that moment heaven was opened, and he saw the Spirit of God descending like a dove and lighting on him. And a voice from heaven said, "This is my Son, whom I love; with him I am well pleased." (Matthew 3:16-17)

Modern readers skate over this account as if it is merely a postscript to Jesus' baptism. Yet what happened there was of earth-shattering importance. With the baptism of Jesus there was an opening of heaven itself. A visual sign of His glory was given in the form of the descending dove. Added to this was the audible voice of God. Imagine the reaction of the bystanders. Only three times does the New Testament record that God spoke audibly.

The baptism of Jesus marks a turning point in His life. He now leaves the carpenter shop to assume the responsibilities of His earthly ministry. Before His actual ministry can begin, however, He must first undergo the testing in the wilderness. We will examine that episode in the next chapter.

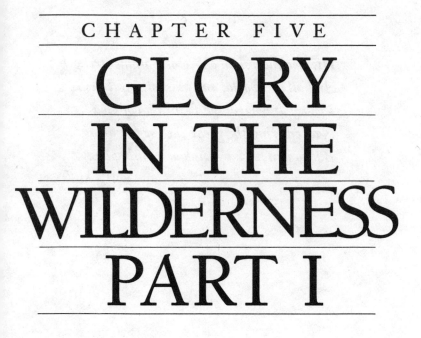

CHAPTER FIVE

GLORY IN THE WILDERNESS

PART I

His weakness shall o'ercome Satanic strength
And all the world, and mass of sinful flesh . . .
Victory and Triumph to the Son of God
Now ent'ring the great duel, not of arms
But to vanquish by wisdom hellish wiles.

JOHN MILTON

IMMEDIATELY FOLLOWING His baptism, Jesus was subjected to the most rigorous test ever to befall a human being. This event was ordained by God. It was a necessary task for Jesus to perform in order to qualify for His role as our Redeemer. Luke introduces this episode by saying: "Jesus, full of the Holy Spirit, returned from the Jordan and was led by the Spirit in the desert" (Luke 4:1).

Jesus was directed by the Spirit to the place of His trial. It was in the wilderness of Judea. This wilderness is one of the most desolate areas on earth, a rare combination of mountains and desert. The inhabitants of this forbidding environment include scorpions, snakes, and a few species of birds. For the most part the landscape is utterly barren.

I have vivid memories of a bus trip from Jerusalem to the Dead Sea. This journey included passing through the Judean wilderness. As I looked out of the bus window I was gripped by a sense of foreboding. I imagined a man walking alone into the most remote portion of this place. I shivered to think of being alone there.

Why would God ever lead anyone to such a place to be exposed to temptation? The reason for the temptation of Christ must be found in His role as the New or Second Adam. As we have seen earlier, Jesus took upon Himself all the obligations imposed by God's covenant with man. The first covenant was the covenant with Adam.

The covenant of creation is a universal covenant. Every human being is included in the creation covenant. There is no escape from the obligations imposed by it. Every person has a copy of its stipulations written on his heart. Paul stated it this way:

When Gentiles, who do not have the law, do by nature things required by the law, they are a law for themselves, even though they do not have the law, since they show that the requirements of the law are written on their hearts, their consciences also bearing witness, and their thoughts now accusing, now even defending them. (Romans 2:14-15)

Men may deny the existence of God or refuse to honor Him. But man's unbelief or disobedience do nothing to harm the being of God. God exists whether or not people believe in Him. His covenant is binding even though we choose to ignore it. Every human being is inescapably bound to a covenant relationship with God. The covenant God made with Adam He made with the representative of the entire human race.

In the covenant with Adam, the blessings of God were promised for obedience and the curse for disobedience. Adam was then put on trial. When he sinned against God, he violated the covenant and brought disaster upon the whole human race.

The crucial point of Adam's temptation is seen in that he was not acting as an isolated individual. He acted on behalf of all mankind. The consequence visited upon the human race because of Adam's failure is summarized by Paul:

Just as sin entered the world through one man, and death through sin, and in this way death came to all men, because all sinned—for before the law was given, sin was in the world. But sin is not taken into account when there is no law. Nevertheless, death reigned from the time of Adam to the time of Moses, even over those who did not sin by breaking a command, as did Adam, who was a pattern of the one to come.

But the gift is not like the trespass. For if the many died by the trespass of the one man, how much more did God's grace and the gift that came by the grace of the one man, Jesus Christ, overflow to the many! Again, the gift of God is not like the result of the one man's sin: The judgment followed one sin and brought condemnation, but the gift followed many trespasses and brought justification. For if, by the trespass of the one man, death reigned through that one man, how much more will those who receive God's abundant provision of grace and of the gift of righteousness reign in life through the one man, Jesus Christ.

Consequently, just as the result of one trespass was condemnation for all men, so also the result of one act of righteousness was justification that brings life for all men. For just as through the disobedience of the one man the many were made sinners, so also through the obedience of the one man the many will be made righteous. (Romans 5:12-19)

Here Paul contrasts the failure of Adam with the victory of Christ, the New Adam. Both Adam and Jesus served as universal covenant representatives. Both were subjected to a test.

The work of Christ involved much more than offering an atonement to pay for the sins of His people. He also had to fulfill all righteousness in order to merit the rewards of the covenant for Himself and those whom He represented. For Christ to be our Savior He not only had to die for our sins, but He also had to live a life of obedience that He might be our righteousness.

The Bible tells us that Christ was like us at every point, except one: He was without sin. The author of Hebrews writes:

We do not have a high priest who is unable to sympathize with our weaknesses, but we have one who has been tempted in every way, just as we are—yet was without sin. (Hebrews 4:14-15)

The sinlessness of Jesus is crucial to our salvation. His sinlessness includes not only freedom from active sin but also freedom from original sin. The concept of original sin is important to our understanding of the temptation of Christ.

When theologians speak of original sin, they are not referring to the first sin committed by Adam and Eve. They are referring to the result of that first transgression, the fallen nature that is passed on to the human race. Original sin is not an act; it is a condition. It is a condition of fallen man that is described in the Bible as being "in the flesh." This means that as fallen creatures we are in bondage to sin, having a heart and will that are inclined toward disobedience.

What was the condition of Jesus when He faced His trial? As the New Adam facing a new probation, Jesus was born without original sin. Jesus possessed the same moral state that Adam did before the Fall. Jesus had the ability to sin and the ability to not sin. Like the first Adam, He had a choice.

Some Christians ask, Was it really possible for Jesus to

have sinned? If it was humanly impossible for Jesus to have sinned, then was His test merely a charade? Some insist that since God cannot possibly sin and that Jesus was God incarnate, then it was impossible for Jesus to have sinned. The issue here focuses on how we understand the two natures of Christ. Obviously the divine nature of Jesus does not have the ability to sin. But with respect to the role of Jesus as the New Adam we are concerned with His human nature. In Jesus the divine nature was united with an *unfallen* human nature. That means that the human nature did not have original sin. The human nature, like Adam before the Fall, had the ability to sin and the ability to not sin.

We can say then that, touching His human nature, it was possible for Him to sin. We must insist that the human nature of Christ had the ability to sin just as Adam did. However, we must also remember that this human nature was in intimate union with the divine nature, a union that Adam did not possess.

The temptation of Christ was not an empty charade. The full force of hell was levied against the human nature of Jesus. In His human nature He suffered under the burden of hunger, loneliness, and all the other perils of the wilderness.

In order to gain a picture of the severity of the test given to Jesus, it may be helpful to note some contrasts between His experience and Adam's.

The testing place of Adam was Eden, a paradise, a lush garden with beautiful surroundings and abundant food. Adam was tested on a full stomach; Jesus was tested in the middle of a long fast.

Adam had Eve. We must remember that his wife was the special creation of God to be a perfect companion. Adam and Eve were subjected to the assault of evil against them while they had each other from whom to gain support. Jesus faced the tempter alone.

For many people, solitude is no barrier to sin. It is usually an opportunity for sinning, with the hope that the sin will go unnoticed. The Bible speaks of those sins done in private under the cover of darkness. The presence of others who can witness our behavior often serves as a restraint. But Jesus was alone.

Another contrast between the first Adam and the Second Adam was the absence and the presence of the *custom* of sin. When Adam and Eve were tested, there was no cultural climate of sin. There was no sin at all. It was a cultural environment of pristine purity. When Jesus entered into His temptation, He did so in a world that was accustomed to sin. It was an environment that thought little or nothing about making concessions to human weakness. It was a culture that accepted a level of behavior far short of perfection. Jesus had to face the argument of "What's the harm of one little concession to evil? Everybody else is doing it." The standard Jesus was called to uphold was a standard that no human being had been able to achieve.

We are daily drawn to standards that are less than the standards of God. We embrace a moral relativism in which we judge ourselves comparatively to others. As long as we can point to others more sinful than ourselves, we can ease our consciences a bit. But for Jesus in the wilderness there was no hope that God was going to judge Him on a curve. He was given the mission of achieving perfect obedience. Nothing less would suffice if He was to qualify as the Lamb without blemish.

When the Letter to the Hebrews declares that "we do not have a high priest who cannot sympathize with our weaknesses," it is reminding us that our Savior was subjected to a temptation that was real. Jesus felt the force of the assault of Satan in the very depths of His humanity.

In addition to the question of the state in which Jesus was tempted, we must also consider the test itself. We will examine this in the next chapter.

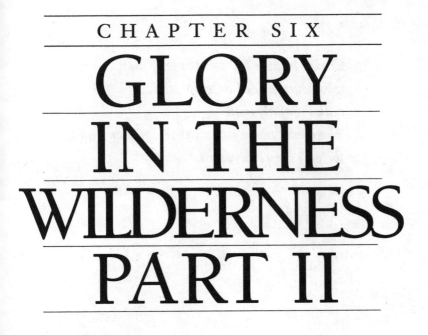

CHAPTER SIX

GLORY IN THE WILDERNESS

PART II

Christ, because He was the only man
who never yielded to temptation,
is also the only man
who knows to the full what temptation means—
the only complete realist.

C. S. LEWIS

W E HAVE EXAMINED the theological questions concerning the temptation of Jesus. Now we will focus on the assault Satan used to entice Jesus. We will follow Luke's account of the event:

Jesus, full of the Holy Spirit, returned from the Jordan and was led by the Spirit in the desert, where for forty days he was tempted by the devil. He ate nothing during those days, and at the end of them he was hungry.

The devil said to him, "If you are the Son of God, tell this stone to become bread."

Jesus answered, "It is written: 'Man does not live on bread alone.'"

The devil led him up to a high place and showed him in an instant all the kingdoms of the world. And he said to him, "I will give you all their authority and splendor, for it has been given to me, and I can give it to anyone I want to. So if you worship me, it will all be yours."

Jesus answered, "It is written: 'Worship the Lord your God and serve him only.'"

The devil led him to Jerusalem and had him stand on the highest point of the temple. "If you are the Son of God," he said, "throw yourself down from here. For it is written:

'He will command his angels concerning you
to guard you carefully;
they will lift you up in their hands,
so that you will not strike your foot against a stone.'"

Jesus answered, "It says: 'Do not put the Lord your God to the test.'" (Luke 4:1-12)

The first approach that Satan made to Jesus involved an enticement to turn stones into bread. Jesus had gone forty days without food.

Satan is described in Scripture as being subtle and wily. When he first appears in Genesis as the serpent who tempted Eve, he is described in these terms: "The serpent was more crafty than any of the wild animals the LORD God had made. He said to the woman, 'Did God really say, "You must not eat from any tree in the garden"?'" (Genesis 3:1). The subtlety of Satan's temptation is seen in the way he phrases his enticement. He says to Jesus, "If you are the Son of God, tell this stone to become bread." The key word is *if*. The devil is subtly raising a question about Jesus' identity.

The temptation has a double force. The first force deals overtly with Jesus' hunger. In His human nature Jesus obviously felt the desire for food. A hungry man's desire for food is no sin. The physical appetite itself has no negative moral value. But it is a desire. Desire is a formidable incitement to many kinds of sins. We must consider James's explanation of temptation at this point:

When tempted, no one should say, "God is tempting me." For God cannot be tempted by evil, nor does he tempt anyone; but each one is tempted when, by his own evil desire, he is dragged away and enticed. Then, after desire has conceived, it gives birth to sin; and sin, when it is full-grown, gives birth to death. (James 1:13-15)

James insists that God is never the tempter to evil. God tests people, but He never tempts them to sin. To be sure, it was God the Holy Spirit who sent Jesus into the wilderness to be tested. But the Spirit was not the agent of the temptation itself. That was the work of Satan.

James describes how temptation occurs: "But each one is tempted when, by his own evil desire, he is dragged away and enticed. Then after desire has conceived, it gives birth to sin." Here James draws an analogy from the birth process. Just as birth is the culmination of conception, so sin is the culmination of an evil desire. Actual sin has its conception in the evil desires of the heart.

How does this apply to the temptation of Christ? Did Jesus have to struggle against His evil desires in order to avoid giving birth to sin? (This is the scandalous suggestion made infamous in the film version of *The Last Temptation of Christ*.)

It is crucial to remember that when James gives this account of how evil desires lead to actual sin, he is describing the situation that applies to fallen mankind. James fully understood that evil desires themselves are also under the judgment of God as they belong to the complex of sinfulness. For Jesus to be free of original sin meant that He was also free of evil desires. One evil desire in the heart of Jesus would have been enough to disqualify Him from being the Savior.

But if Jesus had no evil desires, how could He have been tempted? Here we must distinguish between two types of temptation, internal temptation and external temptation. Internal temptation has to do with the struggle with evil desires that James discusses. External temptation has to do with enticements that come to us from someone or something outside of ourselves. For example, someone comes to me and says, "Let's rob a bank tonight and get rich." All things being equal, I may have a desire to be rich, but I have no desire to rob a bank. Such a suggestion may not incite any evil desires within me. The temptation is purely external. It is an incitement to sin brought to me from someone external to me.

Jesus' temptation was purely external. He merely had to listen to Satan offer external incitements to sin without having to endure the inward struggle with evil desires. Jesus had no inward evil desires. But He did have an inward desire. He was hungry. He had a desire for food, which was not sinful. Satan sought to entice Jesus to fulfill a legitimate desire by using illegitimate means. Wanting bread would have been no sin, but turning the stone into bread would have been. The subtle ploy of Satan failed. Jesus no doubt had a desire for food, but He had an even greater desire for obedience. His meat and His drink was to do the will of His Father.

Satan also attempted to raise questions in Jesus' mind about the trustworthiness of the Word of God. I see this as being of the very essence of the temptation.

The words "If you are the Son of God" subtly raise the issue of Jesus' status with the Father. It is as if Satan was saying, "How could you be the Son of God and be in this place under these conditions? Isn't this beneath the dignity of the Son of God? Would God abandon

His Son to this desolation? If you really are the Son of God then surely you are allowed to fix yourself some breakfast from these stones."

Remember the last portion of the record of Jesus' baptism. The heavens opened, a dove descended, and God spoke audibly. The message God gave from heaven was that Jesus was His beloved Son. That is, the last words Jesus heard from the Father before He entered into His temptation were the words declaring Him to be the Son of God.

The attack of Satan focused upon the trustworthiness of the Word of God. He was raising questions about Jesus' trust in what God had declared.

This is reminiscent of the temptation the serpent brought to Adam and Eve.

The serpent was more crafty than any of the wild animals the LORD God had made. He said to the woman, "Did God really say, 'You must not eat from any tree in the garden'?"

The woman said to the serpent, "We may eat fruit from the trees in the garden, but God did say, 'You must not eat fruit from the tree that is in the middle of the garden, and you must not touch it, or you will die.'"

"You will not surely die," the serpent said to the woman. (Genesis 3:1-4)

Here Satan begins his temptation by asking a question, "Did God really say . . . ?" The initial satanic assault upon the human race began with a question concerning the trustworthiness of God. Satan knew very well that God had not told His creatures that they were not allowed to eat of any of the trees in the garden. In fact,

God had said: " 'You are free to eat from any tree in the garden'" (Genesis 2:16). Eve was quick to defend God at this point:

The woman said to the serpent, "We may eat fruit from the trees in the garden, but God did say, 'You must not eat fruit from the tree that is in the middle of the garden, and you must not touch it, or you will die.'" (Genesis 3:2-3)

The serpent suggested that if God put any restrictions on His creatures then they were not really free at all. The French existentialist philosopher Jean-Paul Sartre has argued that only autonomy is true freedom—total freedom from all authority. This is similar to the complaint parents frequently hear from children. If six days in a row we allow our children to do what they request and on the seventh day we turn them down, we hear these words of protest: "You never let me do anything!" Whatever the subtlety was in the serpent's opening gambit, he quickly moved to a direct, unsubtle contradiction of God:

"You will not surely die," the serpent said to the woman. *"For God knows that when you eat of it your eyes will be opened, and you will be like God, knowing good and evil."* (Genesis 3:4-5)

"You will not surely die." Here Satan directly challenges the truthfulness of God. Eve was faced with a momentous issue, the issue of determining who was telling the truth. Should she trust God, or should she surrender to the skepticism of the serpent?

The plunge of the human race into evil was precipitated by a rejection of the trustworthiness of God.

Satan's ploy worked effectively with Adam and Eve. He used the same tactic with Jesus.

When Satan challenged Jesus to turn the stones into bread in the first temptation, Jesus responded by quoting Scripture: "Jesus answered, 'It is written: "Man does not live on bread alone"'" (Luke 4:4). Here Jesus quotes directly from the Old Testament. The full text reads:

He humbled you, causing you to hunger and then feeding you with manna, which neither you nor your fathers had known, to teach you that man does not live on bread alone but on every word that comes from the mouth of the LORD. (Deuteronomy 8:3)

Jesus' response not only involved a quotation from Scripture, but it was a Scripture that underscored the necessity of living by trust in the Word of God. It is as though Jesus said to Satan, "I don't need to eat bread to know that I am the Son of God. My Father has declared it. I live by every word that proceeds from His mouth." When the first temptation failed, Satan moved to another one:

The devil led him up to a high place and showed him in an instant all the kingdoms of the world. And he said to him, "I will give you all their authority and splendor, for it has been given to me, and I can give it to anyone I want to. So if you worship me, it will all be yours."

Jesus answered, "It is written: 'Worship the LORD your God and serve him only.'" (Luke 4:5-8)

This temptation focuses upon Jesus' mission. Jesus had been promised kingship and all the authority and glory that goes with being the King of kings. But first He had to fulfill the mission of the Suffering Servant of Israel. His kingdom was to be reached though humiliation, suffering, and death. Now Satan offered Him the kingdom without having to pay the price of humiliation. Here the prize is sheer glory without suffering. All Jesus had to do was give the evil prince of this world a moment of worship. Perhaps all Satan wanted was a bow of the knee, a slight genuflection. That would have satisfied him for with the slightest act of obeisance to him the obedience of Jesus would have been compromised.

Again Jesus responded to the temptation with a citation from Scripture: "Jesus answered, 'It is written: "Worship the Lord your God and serve him only"'" (Luke 4:8). For Jesus to submit to Satan would be a violation of the Word of God. Rather than break the commands of the God, Jesus chose the way of suffering and humiliation.

In the third temptation Satan himself appeals to Scripture. He seeks to turn the Word of God as a tool for his own wicked devices:

The devil led him to Jerusalem and had him stand on the highest point of the temple. "If you are the Son of God," he said, "throw yourself down from here. For it is written:
'He will command his angels concerning you
*   to guard you carefully;*
they will lift you up in their hands,
*   so that you will not strike your foot against a stone.'"*
Jesus answered, "It says: 'Do not put the Lord your God to the test.'" (Luke 4:9-12)

Satan appeals to Scripture and suggests that Jesus prove the Scriptures to be true by putting them to the test. At this point Jesus rebukes Satan for setting Scripture against Scripture. Satan had suggested a method of verifying the truthfulness of God's Word by using means that were disallowed by God's Word. Satan again returns to the question of Jesus' Sonship. "If You are the Son of God . . ." Jesus refused to compromise the Scripture. He lived out His own teaching that the Scripture cannot be broken.

Jesus also gives us a lesson in hermeneutics here. He would have nothing to do with a biblical interpretation that would consider one passage in isolation from the whole. He would not interpret one passage of Scripture so as to bring it in conflict with another passage.

With Jesus' victory in the third temptation, Satan left Him alone, at least for the time being. Matthew gives us a marvelous piece of additional information: "Then the devil left him, and angels came and attended him" (Matthew 4:11). Satan had just sought to entice Jesus to prove that angels would take care of Him in a crisis. No angels were visible at the time of the temptation. Yet the moment Jesus resisted the temptation, the angels manifested themselves and ministered to His needs. His moment of triumph over the assault of Satan was coupled with a momentary taste of glory, indicated by the presence of the ministering angels. The Son of God was fed and nourished. He was now ready to embark upon His earthly ministry.

CHAPTER SEVEN

GLORY AT THE WEDDING

Miracles and truth are necessary because the whole man must be convinced in body and soul.

BLAISE PASCAL

JESUS' LIFE was a blaze of miracles. His miracles are important not only because of the benefits people received from them, but also because of what they indicate about Jesus Himself.

Before we examine the first of Jesus' recorded miracles, we must first look at the role they play in general. Some argue that the purpose of miracles is to demonstrate the existence of God. But this reverses the role miracles play in the Bible. Before a miracle can be perceived as a miracle, the existence of God must be established first. It is the existence of God that makes miracles possible in the first place.

The chief purpose of miracles in the Bible is to indicate God's stamp of approval upon His messengers. The miracle certifies a person as a genuine agent of revelation. Nicodemus greeted Jesus by saying:

"Rabbi, we know you are a teacher who has come from God. For no one could perform the miraculous signs you are doing if God were not with him." (John 3:2)

There are many who believe that Nicodemus's judgment in this case was incorrect. He said, "No one can do these signs that you do unless God is with him." Many believe that the Bible proves Nicodemus wrong, at least to a point. They are aware of the biblical warnings against the lying signs and wonders of Satan and his agents.

The question is, can a person opposed to God perform

actual miracles? Are Satan's "miracles" called "lying signs and wonders" because they are real miracles with a false message or because they are false or counterfeit miracles altogether? Are they merely clever tricks like those performed by accomplished magicians, or does Satan have power over nature?

This is not the place to embark on a lengthy exploration of these questions. I have dealt with them more extensively in *The Mystery of the Holy Spirit*. I will only comment here to say that in my judgment Nicodemus's observation is sound. It is consistent with the fact that Scripture does appeal to miracles as proof of divine endorsement and certification, which God would never grant to Satan or to false prophets.

The author of Hebrews writes:

We must pay more careful attention, therefore, to what we have heard, so that we do not drift away. For if the message spoken by angels was binding, and every violation and disobedience received its just punishment, how shall we escape if we ignore such a great salvation? This salvation, which was first announced by the Lord, was confirmed to us by those who heard him. God also testified to it by signs, wonders and various miracles, and gifts of the Holy Spirit distributed according to his will. (Hebrews 2:1-4)

So God uses miraculous signs to certify His messengers. The presence of a miracle in a person's life or ministry does not prove that he is divine; it does prove, however, that he is certified by God. Other biblical characters performed miracles besides

Jesus—for example, Moses and Paul. These miracles were signs of God's certification:

Moses answered, "What if they do not believe me or listen to me and say, 'The LORD did not appear to you'?"
    Then the LORD said to him, "What is that in your hand?"
    "A staff," he replied.
    The LORD said, "Throw it on the ground."
    Moses threw it on the ground and it became a snake, and he ran from it. Then the LORD said to him, "Reach out your hand and take it by the tail." So Moses reached out and took hold of the snake and it turned back into a staff in his hand. "This," said the LORD, "is so that they may believe that the LORD, the God of their fathers—the God of Abraham, the God of Isaac and the God of Jacob—has appeared to you." (Exodus 4:1-5)

In his Gospel, John uses the word *signs* to indicate the miracles of Jesus. The word itself calls attention to the purpose of miracles. Miracles are called signs because they signify something. They point beyond the works themselves to something else, something greater. The signs of Jesus point to the true identity of Jesus. The first sign was at the wedding at Cana.

On the third day a wedding took place at Cana in Galilee. Jesus' mother was there, and Jesus and his disciples had also been invited to the wedding. When the wine was gone, Jesus' mother said to him, "They have no more wine."
    "Dear woman, why do you involve me?" Jesus replied, "My time has not yet come." (John 2:1-4)

A wedding feast in ancient Palestine was more elaborate than our modern wedding receptions. They lasted for several days, usually seven. It was the responsibility of

91

the host to make sure that he had enough provisions to last for the entire period. It was a great embarrassment to fall short of food or drink in the midst of the feast.

Mary, the mother of Jesus, noticing the host's plight, brought it to the attention of Jesus. Jesus' reply to her sounds insensitive and harsh. That he called His mother "woman" was a title of high respect, not a curt response. There is a thinly veiled rebuke, however. The answer He gives is tantamount to a refusal, though He goes on to perform the merciful act. Perhaps Jesus read in His mother's words an implied desire for Jesus not only to help the host but to make a dramatic display of His power. If so, then we conclude that Jesus acquiesced to the former while guarding the latter. His words are crucial: "My time has not yet come." What was He referring to? The "time" is used by John to indicate the manifestation of Jesus in glory. It is linked with the death on the cross. On the eve of His crucifixion Jesus prayed to the Father in the upper room:

"Father, the time has come. Glorify your Son, that your Son may glorify you. For you granted him authority over all people that he might give eternal life to all those you have given him." (John 17:1-2)

Jesus indicates that His "time" or His "hour" has come. In his rebuke to His mother at Cana it is probable that He was resisting Mary's impatient attempt to rush the timetable of Jesus' mission. He implied in His rebuke that this was a matter between Him and His heavenly Father.

The following words of Mary may have applied as much to herself as to the servants to whom she spoke: "His mother said to the servants, 'Do whatever he tells you'" (John 2:5). John continues the narrative by supplying the details of the procedures that were followed in accordance with the orders of Jesus:

Nearby stood six stone water jars, the kind used by the Jews for ceremonial washing, each holding from twenty to thirty gallons.

Jesus said to the servants, "Fill the jars with water"; so they filled them to the brim.

Then he told them, "Now draw some out and take it to the master of the banquet."

They did so, and the master of the banquet tasted the water that had been turned into wine. He did not realize where it had come from, though the servants who had drawn the water knew. Then he called the bridegroom aside and said, "Everyone brings out the choice wine first and then the cheaper wine after the guests have had too much to drink; but you have saved the best till now."
(John 2:6-10)

The water jars were large vessels. Together they could hold between 120 and 180 gallons of water. Jesus ordered the servants to fill the stone jars with water. When the water was tasted, it was immediately discovered that the water had turned into wine. This is what is called a miracle of nature—that is, it involved a supernatural change in the nature of a substance.

The new substance was clearly identified by the master of the feast after he had tasted it. Indeed, he identified it as a superior quality wine. It was customary to present the best wine first and to save the inferior grades of wine until later in the feast. So Jesus' provision was not merely adequate—it was more than adequate.

John summarized this event with an important observation: "This, the first of his miraculous signs, Jesus performed in Cana of Galilee" (John 2:11). John declares that in this first sign something was revealed or manifested about Jesus. The word that is used here means to make plain or to make visible. That which had been hidden from view is now openly displayed. What is revealed was the glory of Jesus. Again we see why John chose the word *sign* to describe the miracles of Jesus. These works were not merely miraculous; they were revelatory. They pointed beyond themselves to the glory of the One who performed them.

Signs are nonverbal communication. Though no words are used, a clear message is conveyed. As we communicate with each other on a human level, we do not simply rely upon words; we add voice inflections, gestures, and facial expressions. All of these are important means of nonverbal communication; they support or clarify what the words convey.

In debates with His contemporaries, Jesus appealed to the testimony of His works:

Jesus answered, "I did tell you, but you do not believe. The miracles I do in my Father's name speak for me, but you do not believe because you are not my sheep. My sheep listen to my voice; I know them, and they follow me." (John 10:25-27)

Again He said:

"Do not believe me unless I do what my Father does. But if I do it, even though you do not believe me, believe the

*miracles, that you may know and understand that the
Father is in me, and I in the Father."* (John 10:37-38)

To believe in the miracles is to believe in what the
miracles signify. It is to embrace what the signs make
manifest. John declares that the sign of Cana manifested the glory of Christ. It was this significance that
the disciples realized and then believed in Him. The
sign revealed glory and the manifestation of Christ's
glory provoked the disciples to faith. The disciples
heard the nonverbal testimony of the works of Jesus and
they put their trust in Him.

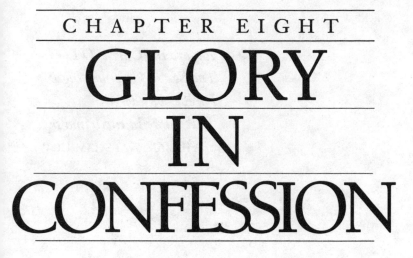

CHAPTER EIGHT

GLORY IN CONFESSION

You are the Christ, O Lord,
The Son of God most high!
Forever be adored
That name in earth and sky.
WILLIAM WALSHAM HOW

J ESUS JOURNEYED WITH His disciples to the region of Caesarea Philippi in the north central section of Galilee, not far from Mount Hermon.[1] This town had been rebuilt by Philip, a son of Herod the Great and half brother of Herod Antipas (who Jesus once referred to as "that fox" [Luke 13:31-32] and who was involved in Jesus' trial [Luke 23:7-12]). Philip had named it Caesarea Philippi in honor of Tiberius Caesar, the Roman emperor.

Why did Jesus retreat to Caesarea Philippi? Probably the trip to Caesarea occurred in the last year of Jesus' life and ministry. Jesus' popularity with the crowds had dwindled, and even some of His disciples had deserted Him. Many were frustrated by Jesus' steadfast refusal to adapt His ministry to the style of conquering king that the public demanded. The Jewish authorities in Jerusalem were hostile toward Him, and Herod Antipas was suspicious of Jesus' possible political aspirations. Merrill Tenney observes:

The Synoptics convey the impression that Jesus tried to stay out of Herod's territory: John indicates that He remained away from Jerusalem until the Feast of Tabernacles

1. Caesarea Philippi is not to be confused with Caesarea, sometimes called Caesarea Maritima, which was one of the largest cities of Judea, built by Herod the Great in honor of Octavian (Augustus). Caesarea Maritima was a major harbor on the seacoast and served as the military and political headquarters of the Roman procurator, Pontius Pilate. Caesarea Philippi was much smaller.

*(John 7:2). One may conclude that the entire summer of
the last year was a period of great uncertainty in which the
popular opinion was fluctuating, favor was diminishing,
and the shadow of the cross was deepening over Jesus'
consciousness."* [2]

It was said that President Lyndon B. Johnson carried
in his pocket the most recent results of public opinion
polls. Some politicians see which way the parade is
marching and then rush to the front of it to assume a
feigned position of leadership.

This was not the tactic of Jesus. Jesus refused to allow
public opinion to steer His ministry. His mandate was
from His Father, and He was zealous to perform it
regardless of the will of the masses.

The experience Jesus had at Caesarea Philippi was a
turning point in His ministry. It was also a turning point
for His disciples.

Confusion reigned regarding His true identity. At
Caesarea Philippi He directed a loaded question to His
disciples: "Who do men say that I, the Son of Man,
am?" (Matthew 16:13). The way Jesus posed this question is unusual. In asking about the popular views of His
identity, Jesus uses His favorite self-designation. He
doesn't merely ask, "Who do they say that I am?"—He
adds "the Son of Man" to His question.

By referring to Himself as the Son of Man, Jesus was
not speaking in a manner of self-effacing humility. The
title "Son of Man" has its roots in the Old Testament

2. Merrill Tenny, *New Testament Times* (Grand Rapids: Eerdmans, 1965),
169.

prophet Daniel who described the figure of the Son of Man as follows:

In my vision at night I looked, and there before me was one like a son of man, coming with the clouds of heaven. He approached the Ancient of Days and was led into his presence. He was given authority, glory and sovereign power; all peoples, nations and men of every language worshiped him. His dominion is an everlasting dominion that will not pass away, and his kingdom is one that will never be destroyed. (Daniel 7:13-14)

By identifying Himself as the Son of Man, Jesus was declaring that He was a heavenly being. The one who later would ascend into heaven was the one who had first descended from heaven. The Son of Man is a figure of glory. He comes to the Ancient of Days with the heavenly clouds of glory. To Him is given glory along with an everlasting dominion and an unconquerable kingdom. The Son of Man is the Old Testament-promised King of Glory.

We might paraphrase Jesus's query in this manner: "Who do people think that I, the King of Glory, am?"

The disciples responded by summarizing the various views of Jesus the public assumed.

They replied, "Some say John the Baptist; others say Elijah; and still others, Jeremiah or one of the prophets." (Matthew 16:14)

Though public opinion was divided, ranging from the reappearance of John the Baptist (who had been beheaded) to the fulfillment of the Old Testament expectation of the return of Elijah, to Jeremiah or some other prophet, there was a common recurring theme: public opinion seemed to fix on the idea that Jesus was some sort of prophet.

Jesus was a prophet, but this was an inadequate designation. He was more than a prophet. And in His role of prophet, Jesus exceeded anything found in the prophetic models of Elijah, Jeremiah, or John the Baptist. Jesus was the Prophet par excellence. He was a prophet without peer. As a prophet, Jesus not only *announced* the Word of God but also *was* the Word of God.

A major concern of Old Testament prophecy was the announcement of the coming of Israel's Messiah. If Jesus were merely another prophet in a long line of prophets, we would expect Him to point to a future Messiah. Jesus did make prophetic utterances about the Messiah, but in so doing He was speaking of Himself.

The question of the coming Messiah is thrust into the core of the discussion at Caesarea Philippi. After patiently hearing what others thought about Him, Jesus posed a second question directed at His own disciples: "But who do you say that I am?" (Matthew 16:15).

Simon Peter, the spokesman for the group, hastened to give reply. His answer to the question stands as the church's first creed. Peter said: "You are the Christ, the Son of the living God." (Matthew 16:16).

Peter's reply is unambiguous. What had been unclear to the public was now crystal clear to Peter. Jesus was the promised Messiah of Israel.

The term "Christ" comes from the Greek *Christos*, meaning "anointed One." It is the New Testament equivalent to the Old Testament Hebrew word *Messiah*. The people had apparently settled for the lesser title of prophet when Jesus failed to live up to their hopes for a political Messiah. What the crowds failed to understand, Peter grasped.

Peter was not satisfied in saying merely, "You are the Christ." He added the words, "the Son of the living God."

We remember that when Jesus asked His first question He had said, "Who do men say that I, the *Son of Man*, am?"

When Peter spoke it was as if He said, "You are indeed the Son of Man, but You are also the Son of God and our Messiah."

In this brief exchange, three titles are ascribed to Jesus: Son of Man, Messiah, Son of God.

Jesus' reply to Peter is often overlooked. I frequently ask my students (who are not looking at the text at the time), "What did Jesus say back to Peter after Peter's confession?" Invariably they jump to a later moment in the discourse and say, "You are Peter, and upon this rock I will build my church." Indeed, Jesus did call Peter the "Rock" (Greek *petros*) on this occasion, but not before saying something else. The moment Jesus heard the words of Peter's confession, He pronounced a benediction upon Peter:

Jesus replied, "Blessed are you, Simon son of Jonah, for this was not revealed to you by man, but by my Father in heaven." (Matthew 16:17)

Before Jesus renamed Simon the "Rock" (Peter), he addressed him by his given name, Simon son of Jonah.

He pronounced Him blessed because he was the recipient of information and understanding that was beyond ordinary human insight.

Scholars speak often of the "Messianic Secret" of Jesus. Because of a wildly distorted view of the Messiah that was widespread, Jesus was careful to conceal His role as Messiah until the time it was appropriate to unveil it. Even in this private time with His disciples, He commanded them "that they should tell no one that He was Jesus the Christ" (Matthew 16:20, NKJV). His words here echo those that He said to the leper He cleansed earlier in His ministry, "See that you tell no one" (Matthew 8:4).

The truth that Simon Peter perceived was a truth made known by special revelation. Herein was the nature of the glorious blessing Peter had received. Peter's blessedness was glorious because what was revealed to him was a glimpse of the glorious character of Jesus.

Yet despite Peter's grasp of Jesus' identity as Messiah, he still did not fully understand the mission of the Messiah. He grasped the glory but missed the humiliation that by divine necessity was attached to it.

Following the benediction, Jesus began to reveal more of what would befall Him:

From that time on Jesus began to explain to his disciples that he must go to Jerusalem and suffer many things at the hands of the elders, chief priests and teachers of the law, and that he must be killed and on the third day be raised to life.

Peter took him aside and began to rebuke him. "Never, Lord!" he said. "This shall never happen to you!"
(Matthew 16:21-22)

Soon after Peter received the blessing of Jesus for his confession of faith, he took Jesus aside to admonish Him. Suddenly the disciple presumed to be above the Master. Peter (failing to live up to his new name) rebuked Jesus for saying that He must suffer and die. Peter had an eye for glory but was blind to the tie of that glory to suffering.

Peter couched his rebuke in these terms: "Far be it from you, Lord; this shall not happen to you!" It is as if he said, "Nothing could be further from the truth than the things You have just declared."

At the very moment Peter admonishes, challenges, and corrects Jesus, he addresses Him as "Lord." He follows his rebuke with an emphatic contradiction of what Jesus had just declared would happen. "This shall not happen to you!" Peter, at this point, uttered with great emphasis a future prophecy that proved to be emphatically false.

Jesus turned and said to Peter, "Get behind me, Satan! You are a stumbling block to me; you do not have in mind the things of God, but the things of men." (Matthew 16:23)

The Gospels record instances when Jesus unleashed harsh and severe rebukes. He called Herod Antipas "that fox." He called the Pharisees snakes and children of hell. But nowhere is He more caustic in His rebukes than when He called Peter "Satan."

We remember that when Satan failed to seduce Jesus he departed from Him "for a season." Satan wanted Jesus to seek glory without pain, kingship without the cross. Satan feared nothing more from Jesus than His death. The worst thing that could happen to Satan was for Jesus to make atonement for the sins of His people.

There is nothing in the text, however, that suggests Peter was overtaken here by satanic possession. He may have echoed the sentiments of Satan and voiced the temptation of Satan, but the words still belonged to Peter. Jesus called Peter "Satan," but he was addressing these words to Peter.

It is astonishing that within a short interval of time Jesus pronounces His blessing on Simon and calls him "the rock" and then pronounces His judgment upon him and calls him "Satan." In His words of benediction Jesus had commended Peter for seeing what flesh and blood could not see, for perceiving what the Father revealed. Now He says, "You are not mindful of the things of God, but the things of men."

So soon after reaching beyond the threshold of flesh and blood to see glory, Peter reverted to the "things of men." He was no longer mindful of the things of God.

In this human encounter we observe how easy it is to fuse a confession of faith with radical error and corruption. Those who have eyes only for glory and ignore the way of the cross do not mind the things of God.

Even today advocates of the so-called "prosperity gospel" declare that God has no part in pain and suffering.

The Messiah is indeed the King of Glory. Yet the King of Glory is the Suffering Servant of Israel. It took Peter a while to learn that. Later he could write to the church:

106

In this you greatly rejoice, though now for a little while you may have had to suffer grief in all kinds of trials. These have come so that your faith—of greater worth than gold, which perishes even though refined by fire—may be proved genuine and may result in praise, glory and honor when Jesus Christ is revealed. (1 Peter 1:6-7)

Again Peter writes:

But even if you should suffer for what is right, you are blessed. (1 Peter 3:14)

CHAPTER NINE
GLORY ON THE MOUNTAIN

O God, who on the holy mount
didst reveal to chosen witnesses
thy well-beloved Son,
wonderfully transfigured,
in raiment and glistening:
Mercifully grant that we,
being delivered from
the disquietude of this world,
may by faith behold the King in his beauty.

THE BOOK OF COMMON PRAYER

PROBABLY THE MOST dazzling breakthrough of the glory of Christ in His entire life took place on the Mount of Transfiguration. The site of this extraordinary event is not known for certain, but it probably took place on Mount Hermon. Mount Hermon, which rises to 9,200 feet, is situated a short distance from Caesarea Philippi. Matthew gives this description:

After six days Jesus took with him Peter, James and John the brother of James, and led them up a high mountain by themselves. There he was transfigured before them. His face shone like the sun, and his clothes became as white as the light. Just then there appeared before them Moses and Elijah, talking with Jesus. (Matthew 17:1-3)

This unveiling of glory was witnessed by only three of the disciples. These three—Peter, James, and John—are unusually designated the "inner core" or "inner circle" of the Twelve.

The text says that Jesus was "transfigured." We may divide this phenomenon into three main stages. First, there is the Transfiguration itself. Second, there is the appearance of Moses and Elijah conversing with Jesus. Third, there is the voice from heaven.

THE TRANSFIGURATION
The word Matthew and Mark use for Transfiguration is a form of the verb *metamorpho*, from which the English

word *metamorphosis* is derived. A metamorphosis is a transformation, a change of form. When the caterpillar goes through metamorphosis, it becomes a butterfly. It indicates a real change in form. (The Greek *morphe* means "shape" or "form.") The noun from which the verb used here derives describes an essential form, not merely a mask or temporary appearance.

The English *Transfiguration* employs the prefix *trans-*, which means "across." A transoceanic voyage travels across the ocean. A transcontinental trip moves across the continent. The English word *transfigure* is an appropriate selection to capture the meaning of the event. A limit or barrier is crossed here. Perhaps we might call it a crossing of the line between natural and supernatural, between the human and the divine.

THE VISIBLE DESCRIPTION

The Gospel writers give a vivid account of what was seen by the disciples.

His face shone like the sun. Both Luke and Matthew record that the face of Jesus began to shine. Matthew compares the radiance of the shining to the intensity of the sun. This experience recalls the experience of Moses, whose face shone on Mount Sinai.

Since Luke adds that Jesus was in a posture of prayer, some suggest that Jesus, like Moses before Him, was *reflecting* the glory of God, in whose presence He was. The shining face, then, is not an indication of Jesus' own deity shining through but merely a human reflection of God's glory.

However, this is not the thrust of the text or of later apostolic testimony. John's prologue speaks of the divine Logos who became incarnate:

The Word became flesh and made his dwelling among us. We have seen his glory, the glory of the One and Only, who came from the Father, full of grace and truth. (John 1:14)

Here the incarnate divine Logos manifests His own unique glory. What John said "we beheld" was not a reflected glory as in the case of Moses but the Word's *own* glory. John speaks of the glory of "the only begotten of the Father"—this "only begotten" puts Christ in a class by Himself.

The Letter to the Hebrews emphasizes the superiority of Christ:

In the past God spoke to our forefathers through the prophets at many times and in various ways, but in these last days he has spoken to us by his Son, whom he appointed heir of all things, and through whom he made the universe. The Son is the radiance of God's glory and the exact representation of his being, sustaining all things by his powerful word. After he had provided purification for sins, he sat down at the right hand of the Majesty in heaven. (Hebrews 1:1-3)

Christ does not merely reflect the brightness of divine glory. He *is* the brightness of divine glory. In this His glory clearly transcends the reflected glory seen on the face of Moses.

That Jesus' face shone like the sun suggests an intensity of dazzling light that is virtually blinding to the eyes, the kind of light that blinded Saul on the road to Damascus.

As he neared Damascus on his journey, suddenly a light from heaven flashed around him. (Acts 9:3)

Later Paul adds:

My companions led me by the hand into Damascus, because the brilliance of the light had blinded me. (Acts 22:11)

For anything to shine like the sun it must emit rays so brilliant as to be painful. James refers to God as the "Father of lights" (1:17), who dwells in "light inaccessible."

His clothes became as white as the light. Matthew says they were "white as the light" (17:2). Luke says "as bright as a flash of lightning" (9:29). Mark says "dazzling white, whiter than anyone in the world could bleach them" (9:3).

We are accustomed to efforts of Madison Avenue advertisers to promote the newest and best laundry detergents. They promise clothes that come out "whiter than white."

There is no such thing as whiter than white. If something is pure white, it allows for no further degree of whiteness. The white of Jesus' garments exceeds that achieved by any earthly cleansing process.

The effort to describe the whiteness of Christ's garments brings to mind novelist Herman Melville's attempt to convey a symbol of God in the white whale, Moby Dick:

White is specially employed in the celebration of the passion of our Lord; though in the vision of St. John, white robes are given to the redeemed, and the four-and-twenty elders stand clothed in white before the great white throne and

*the Holy One that sitteth there white like wool; yet for all
these accumulated associations, with whatever is sweet,
and honorable, and sublime, there yet lurks an elusive
something in the innermost idea of this hue, which strikes
more of panic to the soul than that redness which affrights
in blood.*

Melville later explores the root causes of the panic of
the soul evoked by whiteness:

*But not yet have we solved the incantation of this
whiteness, and learned why it appeals with such power to
the soul; and more strange and far more portentous—why,
as we have seen, it is at once the most meaningful symbol of
spiritual things, nay the very veil of the Christian's Deity;
and yet should be as it is, the intensifying agent in things
the most appealing to mankind.*

Melville understood that the mystery of light itself is
somehow bounded up with the "color" white.

*Is it that by its indefiniteness it shadows forth the heartless
voids and immensities of the universe, and thus stabs us
from behind with the thought of annihilation, when
beholding the white depths of the Milky Way? Or is it, that
as in essence whiteness is not so much a color as the visible
absence of color, and at the same time the concrete of all
colors?*

When Jesus' garments became pure and unspotted
white, it happened in the midst of an overpowering
epiphany of light. The brightness of the light and the
purity of the whiteness of His garments belong together.

In viewing the transfigured clothes of Jesus, the disciples saw the purity of whiteness. Nothing was

absorbed or reflected. The source of the light that radiated from Jesus' garments was not external. The sun in the sky did not produce the effect. The light source was Christ Himself.

What color is a lemon? Is it red? black? white? yellow? Which option did you choose? Surely most people would answer "yellow." In terms of ordinary language that answer would be correct. Technically, however, the answer could be challenged. When I say a lemon *is* yellow do I mean that the color yellow is part of the very essence of the lemon? We know better. Color is not a primary quality of anything. Yellowness is not part of the essence of a lemon. In the dark the lemon is black, just like all other unillumined objects. We see color in objects only by means of how they reflect light from themselves.

Without light there is no color. Light contains within its waves all the hues of the rainbow. When light strikes an object some of the colors are absorbed and others are reflected. We see color as it is reflected by objects.

The sight of Jesus' clothes resembled what we see when we gaze upon an illumined angel on the top of a Christmas tree. The Christmas tree angel has a bulb concealed within it. As the light is turned on and current flows to the bulb, the angel begins to glow. The light is diffused throughout the angel. So the garments of Jesus began to glow in the purity of light that emanated from His divine being.

In Revelation 21 we read the following description of the New Jerusalem:

The city does not need the sun or the moon to shine on it, for the glory of God gives it light, and the Lamb is its lamp. (v. 23)

Again:

They will see his face, and his name will be on their foreheads. There will be no more night. They will not need the light of a lamp or the light of the sun, for the Lord God will give them light. (Revelation 22:4-5)

CONVERSATION WITH MOSES AND ELIJAH

At the Transfiguration, Moses and Elijah appeared, talking with Jesus. Luke adds some important information for the record:

Two men, Moses and Elijah, appeared in glorious splendor, talking with Jesus. They spoke about his departure, which he was about to bring to fulfillment at Jerusalem. (Luke 9:30-31)

Why Moses and Elijah? These two are significant not only because of the mysterious character of their respected departures from earth but because of the roles they played in the Old Testament. Moses was the mediator of the Old Covenant as Jesus is the Mediator of the New Covenant. Elijah, whose return was promised in the last prophecy of the Old Testament (see Malachi 4:5), was one of the most important of a long line of Old Testament prophets. Moses and Elijah together represent the Law and the Prophets. The much-used phrase "the Law and the Prophets" served as a summary for the teaching of God in the Old Testament:

117

So in everything, do to others what you would have them do to you, for this sums up the Law and the Prophets. (Matthew 7:12)

Paul later summarized the gospel by saying:

But now a righteousness from God, apart from law, has been made known, to which the Law and the Prophets testify. (Romans 3:21)

On the Mount of Transfiguration the very incarnation and embodiment of the gospel is witnessed in His glory by the Law (Moses) and the Prophets (Elijah).

One of the ironies of this episode is the presence of Moses. After his task of leading the Israelites through the wilderness, Moses was denied entrance into the Promised Land:

Moses climbed Mount Nebo from the plains of Moab to the top of Pisgah, across from Jericho. There the LORD showed him the whole land—from Gilead to Dan, all of Naphtali, the territory of Ephraim and Manasseh, all the land of Judah as far as the western sea, the Negev and the whole region from the Valley of Jericho, the City of Palms, as far as Zoar. Then the LORD said to him, "This is the land I promised on oath to Abraham, Isaac and Jacob when I said, 'I will give it to your descendants.' I have let you see it with your eyes, but you will not cross over into it." (Deuteronomy 34:1-4)

Moses did not *cross* over into the Promised Land. He did finally get there, however, by another route. He did not transverse the Jordan River during his life on earth. Presumably the route he traveled to the Promised Land was vertical. He didn't cross over into Israel, he came down to Israel from heaven. After many centuries he

118

finally stood inside the Promised Land as he spoke face to face with the Promised One.

It is significant that Luke mentions the topic of conversation that took place between Jesus and Moses and Elijah. They were discussing the impending suffering and death that awaited Jesus in Jerusalem. This discussion stands in stark contrast to the one Jesus had only days earlier with His disciples. Moses and Elijah already understood what the disciples found so difficult to grasp. It was not necessary for Jesus to say to either Moses or Elijah, "Get thee behind me, Satan," as He uttered to Peter.

Luke provides no details concerning the content of the conversation. We may only surmise that Jesus received words of encouragement for His task from the Law and the Prophets.

THE VOICE OUT OF THE CLOUD

As Peter's excitement grew as the spectacle unfolded, he prompted Jesus to make provisions for a lengthy stay in this glory. He said:

"Lord, it is good for us to be here. If you wish, I will put up three shelters—one for you, one for Moses and one for Elijah." (Matthew 17:4)

Luke adds an interesting editorial comment: "not knowing what he said" (Luke 9:33).

There is no record of a reply from Jesus to this suggestion. Peter, in awe before the glory, wanted to prolong the experience. He was not prepared to move from a blessed experience to the redemptive task that lay ahead—a task of humiliation, sacrifice, and pain.

Peter's statement received no immediate reply from Jesus. The answer came from another source:

While he was still speaking, a bright cloud enveloped them, and a voice from the cloud said, "This is my Son, whom I love; with him I am well pleased. Listen to him!"
(Matthew 17:5)

Then the disciples were suddenly engulfed by the glory cloud of God. Presumably while they were enshrouded by the cloud they could see nothing save the refulgence that enveloped them. In this terror-provoking situation the sensory experience moves beyond the visual to the auditory. Now they hear the voice of God the Father. As God spoke from heaven at the baptism of Jesus, so He speaks again, declaring that Jesus is His beloved Son. With the declaration comes a command, a divine imperative: "Listen to him!"

At the sound of God's audible voice the disciples fell on the ground, quaking in terror. It was at this point that Jesus finally spoke to them:

When the disciples heard this, they fell facedown to the ground, terrified. But Jesus came and touched them. "Get up," he said. "Don't be afraid." When they looked up, they saw no one except Jesus. (Matthew 17:6-8)

People long to catch a glimpse of the unveiled glory of God. Yet when it appears we are devastated. Men's deepest hopes give way to trembling before the majesty of God. Consider Habakkuk's reaction when he heard the voice of God he had begged to hear:

I heard and my heart pounded,
my lips quivered at the sound;
decay crept into my bones,
and my legs trembled.

(Habakkuk 3:16)

While they were prone on the ground, Jesus came and touched them. We have no record of the tone of His voice, but we assume it was gentle and comforting: "Get up. Don't be afraid." He spoke as a king speaks to his kneeling subjects. He gives permission to them to stand in His presence, added with the admonition to not be afraid.

Matthew mentions that the disciple's response was to "lift up their eyes." When they did, they saw that as suddenly as the supernatural glory had descended upon them it had departed. Moses and Elijah were gone. Jesus was once more alone with them, appearing as He normally did.

This sovereign moment of the breakthrough of divine glory was over. The Transfiguration—by which the line was crossed between finite and infinite, temporal and eternal, natural and supernatural—was finished. But the memory remained. Jesus again had to instruct them to hold this matter as a closely guarded secret until such time that it might be told:

"Don't tell anyone what you have seen, until the Son of Man has been raised from the dead." (Matthew 17:9)

After the Resurrection, Peter was free to write of this experience. The secret could now be told:

I will make every effort to see that after my departure you will always be able to remember these things.

We did not follow cleverly invented stories when we told you about the power and coming of our Lord Jesus Christ, but we were eyewitnesses of his majesty. For he received honor and glory from God the Father when the voice came to him from the Majestic Glory, saying, "This is my Son, whom I love; with him I am well pleased." We ourselves heard this voice that came from heaven when we were with him on the sacred mountain. (2 Peter 1:15-18)

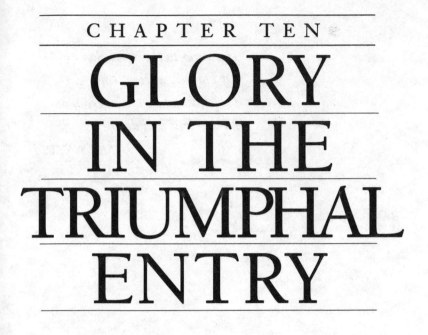

CHAPTER TEN

GLORY IN THE TRIUMPHAL ENTRY

Hosanna to the royal Son
Of David's ancient line!
His natures two, his person one,
Mysterious and divine.

ISAAC WATTS

SOON AFTER the Transfiguration, Jesus and His disciples returned through Galilee and into Judea. The moment of crisis drew near as Jesus prepared to enter Jerusalem. He made careful plans with His disciples concerning the manner of His entry into the city:

As they approached Jerusalem and came to Bethphage and Bethany at the Mount of Olives, Jesus sent two of his disciples, saying to them, "Go to the village ahead of you, and just as you enter it, you will find a colt tied there, which no one has ever ridden. Untie it and bring it here. If anyone asks you, 'Why are you doing this?' tell him, 'The Lord needs it and will send it back here shortly.'"

They went and found a colt outside in the street, tied at a doorway. As they untied it, some people standing there asked, "What are you doing, untying that colt?" They answered as Jesus had told them to, and the people let them go. (Mark 11:1-6)

It was not the usual custom for a pilgrim entering Jerusalem to ride a donkey. Yet Jesus took pains to insure that His entry into the city would be accomplished in that manner. These preparations recall the importance of the great messianic prophecy found in the Old Testament Book of Zechariah:

Rejoice greatly, O Daughter of Zion!
  Shout, Daughter of Jerusalem!
See, your king comes to you,
  righteous and having salvation,

gentle and riding on a donkey,
on a colt, the foal of a donkey.

(Zechariah 9:9)

Though the Old Testament foretells the king coming on a donkey, the episode remained ambiguous to Jesus' contemporaries. Among the Jewish rabbis there were those who believed that the Messiah would arrive in one of two ways depending upon whether or not Israel was worthy of His appearance. If the nation were worthy, the appearance would be on clouds of glory. If the nation was unworthy—unprepared spiritually—then His coming would be by the lowly means of riding on a donkey.

Jesus issued instructions that the animal was to be a colt of a donkey upon which no one had ever sat. These two specifications suggest two different Old Testament considerations. The first is a reference to the patriarchal blessing Jacob gave to his son Judah. It was the tribe of Judah that was promised the kingship:

The scepter will not depart from Judah,
nor the ruler's staff from between his feet,
until he comes to whom it belongs
and the obedience of the nations is his.
He will tether his donkey to a vine,
his colt to the choicest branch;
he will wash his garments in wine,
his robes in the blood of grapes.
His eyes will be darker than wine,
his teeth whiter than milk.

(Genesis 49:10-12)

Here the king from the tribe of Judah is associated with the colt of a donkey. That the donkey should never have been ridden is based upon Old Testament law that animals devoted to sacred tasks must be consecrated, separated from common use. We see this in the Book of Numbers:

The LORD said to Moses and Aaron: "This is a requirement of the law that the LORD has commanded: Tell the Israelites to bring you a red heifer without defect or blemish and that has never been under a yoke." (Numbers 19:1-2)

After the donkey was brought to Jesus, it was draped with the garments of the disciples:

When they brought the colt to Jesus and threw their cloaks over it, he sat on it. Many people spread their cloaks on the road, while others spread branches they had cut in the fields. (Mark 11:7-8)

The draping of the animal with their own garments was an act of honor bestowed upon Jesus by His disciples. Apparently the crowd along the way took up the homage spontaneously by spreading their garments in Jesus' path. This action was reminiscent of the homage paid to Jehu when he became king over Israel:

They hurried and took their cloaks and spread them under him on the bare steps. Then they blew the trumpet and shouted, "Jehu is king!" (2 Kings 9:13)

In John's account of the triumphal entry he mentions the use of palm branches in the acclamation Jesus received from the crowd:

The next day the great crowd that had come for the Feast heard that Jesus was on his way to Jerusalem. They took palm branches and went out to meet him, shouting,
"Hosanna!"

127

"Blessed is he who comes in the name of the Lord!"
"Blessed is the King of Israel!" (John 12:12-13)

Mark does not specify the use of palms but speaks of the people cutting down leafy branches from the trees and spreading them on the road. The people shouted loud cries of acclamation:

Those who went ahead and those who followed shouted,
   "Hosanna!"
"Blessed is he who comes in the name of the Lord!"
"Blessed is the coming kingdom of our father David!"
"Hosanna in the highest!" (Mark 11:9-10)

The use of the cry "Hosanna!" was significant. The term was originally used as a cry to heaven for help. It meant "save us." As language changed, the cry came to signify rejoicing and acclamation. In the English-speaking world it has similarities with the expression "God save the king!" Originally this phrase had a comma—"God, save the king." In this form it is a prayer. Once the comma is dropped, it becomes a shout of praise or honor.

There is also a tradition that indicates palm branches themselves became known as "Hosannas" because they were waved during celebrations. They were often used during the Feast of Tabernacles. Only John's Gospel specifically mentions palm branches. The land around Jerusalem had been denuded of palm trees. It was customary, however, for pilgrims to carry bundles of palm, which were shaken whenever "Hosanna" was said in the Feast of Tabernacles.

There is an unusual scene recorded in the Apocryphal

book of 2 Esdras. The Son of Man appears at the Last Judgment. He distributes palm branches to the martyred saints, signifying their participation with Him in His victory. Though this scene is not a part of the New Testament record, it does correspond with the New Testament theme that believers who are willing to participate in the suffering and the humiliation of Christ will also take part in His final glorious triumph. To share in His humiliation is to have a part in His exaltation. This theme of participation with Christ is exactly what is missing in the events of the week of the triumphal entrance. The same people who were shouting "Hosanna!" and waving palms and other branches were unwilling to identify with Him shortly after at Golgotha. They wanted to participate in the exaltation, but desired no part of the humiliation.

Mark records the content of the shouts and praises of the people:

"Hosanna!"
  "Blessed is he who comes in the name of the Lord!"
  "Blessed is the coming kingdom of our father David!"
  "Hosanna in the highest!" (Mark 11:9-10)

The language of these praises is taken from a series of Old Testament Psalms known as the *Hallel*. (The word *Hallel* is part of the familiar *Hallelujah*—"Praise the Lord.") The Hallel Psalms (Psalms 113–118) were songs of praise that accented the messianic ascent to the Holy City. They were used in the liturgy of the Jews with specific application to Passover and the Feast of Tabernacles.

Psalm 118 contains the following words:

O LORD, save us;
O LORD, grant us success.
Blessed is he who comes in the name of the LORD.
From the house of the LORD we bless you.

(Psalm 118:25-26)

Jesus is hailed with the language of the Psalm as the Blessed One who comes in the name of the Lord. It refers to the Old Testament promise of "The One who is Coming." This has specific reference to the royal Messiah, who comes to restore David's throne. To come "in the name of the Lord" is not merely to come by God's authority; it is to come as a divine revelation by which the Lord makes Himself known.

The crowd repeats the cry "Hosanna" and adds "in the highest. The One who comes is from the house of the Lord." His praises are not only to be sung by the multitudes on earth but also by the host of heaven. "Hosanna in the highest" reflects the jubilation found in Psalm 148:

Praise the LORD.
Praise the LORD from the heavens, praise him in the
  heights above.
Praise him, all his angels, praise him, all his heavenly
  hosts.
Praise him, sun and moon, praise him, all you shining
  stars.
Praise him, you highest heavens and you waters above the
  skies.

(Psalm 148:1-4)

According to Luke's Gospel, not everyone who was

present for the entry in to Jerusalem joined in the celebration. The enemies of Christ were also assembled and took note of what was going on. The Pharisees also shouted to Jesus. Their shouts were not of acclamation, but of rebuke. They demanded that Jesus put a stop to this public display of adulation: "Some of the Pharisees in the crowd said to Jesus, "Teacher, rebuke your disciples!" (Luke 19:39). The religious authorities demanded that Jesus quell the outburst of His disciples. Jesus refused to obey their command: "'I tell you,' he replied, 'if they keep quiet, the stones will cry out'" (Luke 19:40). Jesus declares that it is impossible to keep the earth quiet about His messianic vocation. If the people are silent, there will be a cry from the inanimate objects of nature. The creation cannot deny what the Pharisees are willing to deny. The Messiah of Israel is no mere earthly king. He is a cosmic king. His domain is the entire order of His own creation. Those elements of creation that are mute will be moved to shouting if the lips of men are sealed.

The rabbis had taught that the earth itself bears witness against the evil of man. They specifically declared that the stones of the earth could cry out against those who do evil. Perhaps this is based upon the testimony of Genesis regarding the first act of homicide:

Now Cain said to his brother Abel, "Let's go out to the field." And while they were in the field, Cain attacked his brother Abel and killed him.

Then the LORD said to Cain, "Where is your brother Abel?"

*"I don't know," he replied. "Am I my brother's keeper?"
The LORD said, "What have you done? Listen! Your
brother's blood cries out to me from the ground."* (Genesis
4:8-10)

The evil is attested by the blood of Abel on the
ground. God speaks of Abel's blood that "cries out to
me from the ground." The blood cannot be silent. It
renders loud testimony to the guilt of Cain.

The reference to the stones of the earth also echoes
the rebuke John the Baptist leveled against the Pharisees and Sadducees:

*But when he saw many of the Pharisees and Sadducees
coming to where he was baptizing, he said to them: "You
brood of vipers! Who warned you to flee from the coming
wrath? Produce fruit in keeping with repentance. And do
not think you can say to yourselves, 'We have Abraham as
our father.' I tell you that out of these stones God can raise
up children for Abraham."* (Matthew 3:7-9)

That the whole creation has a stake in Jesus' kingship
is underscored by the cosmic scope of His redemption.
The apostle Paul declares:

*Our present sufferings are not worth comparing with the
glory that will be revealed in us. The creation waits in
eager expectation for the sons of God to be revealed. For the
creation was subjected to frustration, not by its own choice,
but by the will of the one who subjected it, in hope that the
creation itself will be liberated from its bondage to decay
and brought into the glorious freedom of the children of
God.*

*We know that the whole creation has been groaning
as in the pains of childbirth right up to the present time.
Not only so, but we ourselves, who have the firstfruits*

132

of the Spirit, groan inwardly as we wait eagerly for our adoption as sons, the redemption of our bodies. (Romans 8:18-23)

Luke tells us that as Jesus entered the city to the tumultuous welcome of the people, His own spirit was not festive. When He saw the Holy City, He wept over it and pronounced a prophetic oracle of doom:

As he approached Jerusalem and saw the city, he wept over it and said, "If you, even you, had only known on this day what would bring you peace—but now it is hidden from your eyes. The days will come upon you when your enemies will build an embankment against you and encircle you and hem you in on every side. They will dash you to the ground, you and the children within your walls. They will not leave one stone on another, because you did not recognize the time of God's coming to you." (Luke 19:41-44)

At the very moment that the crowds are hailing Him as the one who comes from God, Jesus is aware that they did not really understand who He was or what His mission involved. He understood that His redemptive task was still hidden from their eyes. They celebrated peace but knew nothing of the meaning of peace. For the ultimate peace to be established Jesus had to die as an atonement for His people's sins. His words came true within decades when the Roman legions entered Jerusalem and leveled the city, slaughtering a million Jews and tearing the temple down.

The king of Israel had arrived in Jerusalem. The Son of David had made His messianic office now a public matter. The initial welcome of the crowds was enthusiastic. Yet the weeping of Jesus was an ominous portent of what was shortly to come to pass. The Passover was rapidly approaching and the paschal lamb was being prepared for the slaughter.

CHAPTER ELEVEN

GLORY IN THE UPPER ROOM

I rejoice at your holy banquet.
All is in you, which I can and should desire.
You are my salvation and redemption,
hope and strength, honor and glory.

THE IMITATION OF CHRIST

WHAT WAS the birthday of the Christian church? When does the period of the New Testament actually begin? Various answers are given to these questions. Some point to Pentecost as the birthday of the church. Others point to Easter or to the Crucifixion. I am convinced that the New Testament church was born in the upper room when Jesus celebrated the Last Supper with His disciples. In terms of redemptive history this episode is of crucial importance.

Just as Jesus had directed His disciples earlier to make preparations for His triumphal entry into Jerusalem, now He gives them instructions to prepare a place for them to celebrate the Passover together:

Then came the day of Unleavened Bread on which the Passover lamb had to be sacrificed. Jesus sent Peter and John, saying, "Go and make preparations for us to eat the Passover."

"Where do you want us to prepare for it?" they asked.

He replied, "As you enter the city, a man carrying a jar of water will meet you. Follow him to the house that he enters, and say to the owner of the house, 'The Teacher asks: Where is the guest room, where I may eat the Passover with my disciples?' He will show you a large upper room, all furnished. Make preparations there."

They left and found things just as Jesus had told them. So they prepared the Passover. (Luke 22:7-13)

It was the day of Unleavened Bread. By noon of this

137

day there was to be no leaven in the houses of Jews. The unleavened loaves were being prepared for the Passover. Between two-thirty and six o'clock the paschal lambs were slaughtered and made ready for the Passover. The Passover itself began after sunset. Jesus and His disciples had been spending their nights either in Bethany or on the Mount of Olives. In order to celebrate the Passover they had to secure quarters within Jerusalem. As a result Jesus instructed His disciples to make the necessary arrangements including accommodations in the upper room. Luke continues his narrative:

When the hour came, Jesus and his apostles reclined at the table. And he said to them, "I have eagerly desired to eat this Passover with you before I suffer. For I tell you, I will not eat it again until it finds fulfillment in the kingdom of God."

After taking the cup, he gave thanks and said, "Take this and divide it among you. For I tell you I will not drink again of the fruit of the vine until the kingdom of God comes."

And he took bread, gave thanks and broke it, and gave it to them, saying, "This is my body given for you; do this in remembrance of me."

In the same way, after the supper he took the cup, saying, "This cup is the new covenant in my blood, which is poured out for you." (Luke 22:14-20)

Jesus declared to His disciples that He had a strong desire to eat the Passover with them. He indicates to them that it is the last time He will celebrate this monumental redemptive event with them in this world. This is not only Jesus' last Passover; it is the last Passover celebrated under the old covenant. In the midst of this celebration Jesus transformed it from an Old Testament ceremony to a New Testament ceremony. That which the Passover recalled and also foreshadowed was about to reach its ultimate fulfillment.

In the midst of the Passover celebration Jesus changed the liturgy. When He broke the bread and distributed it among His disciples He declared, "This is my body which is given for you; do this in remembrance of me." He then attached a new significance to the wine that was being used. He said, "This cup is the new covenant in my blood, which is shed for you." On this occasion Jesus' words were radical. He consciously used covenant language. He was instituting a New Covenant.

Like covenants in the past, this New Covenant was to be a blood covenant, shared by all who participated in the rite. Jesus now associated the drinking of the wine with the new covenant that was to be established by the shedding of His blood. He was the new paschal lamb, the lamb that would be slain once for all.

In the original Passover experience of Israel, it was the blood of lambs that marked the way of escape from death. The Book of Exodus records the event:

Then Moses summoned all the elders of Israel and said to them, "Go at once and select the animals for your families and slaughter the Passover lamb. Take a bunch of hyssop, dip it into the blood in the basin and put some of the blood on the top and on both sides of the doorframe. Not one of you shall go out the door of his house until morning. When the LORD goes through the land to strike down the Egyptians, he will see the blood on the top and sides of the doorframe and will pass over that doorway, and he will not permit the destroyer to enter your houses and strike you down.

Obey these instructions as a lasting ordinance for you and your descendants. When you enter the land that the LORD will give you as he promised, observe this ceremony. And when your children ask you, 'What does this ceremony mean to you?' then tell them, 'It is the Passover sacrifice to the LORD, who passed over the houses of the Israelites in Egypt and spared our homes when he struck down the Egyptians.'" Then the people bowed down and worshiped. (Exodus 12:21-27)

As the people of Israel escaped the wrath of the destroyer because their doors were marked by the blood of lambs, so now it is the blood of Christ that marks those who escape from the wrath of God.

When Jesus attaches new meaning to the Passover, He does not repudiate the Old Covenant. Rather, He brings it to fulfillment. His profound respect for the Old Covenant is not only witnessed by His behavior throughout His earthly ministry but is underscored by His deep desire to celebrate the Passover with His disciples.

The New Covenant does not appear unrelated to the Old. It grows out of and completes the Old Covenant. Yet the clear point of transition between the two is seen in these events in the upper room. The new meaning is declared.

For covenants in the Old Testament to be binding upon their adherents, they had to be ratified in blood. The ratification of the New Covenant does not take place in the upper room. The ratification of the New

Covenant occurs when Jesus actually sheds His blood upon the cross.

John supplies much more information about what transpired in the upper room than do the other Gospels. Included in John's record is the episode of Jesus washing the disciples feet. Also, John includes the longest discourse found anywhere in Scripture about the Holy Spirit. Jesus makes the following promises to His disciples about the coming of the Holy Spirit:

"And I will ask the Father, and he will give you another Counselor to be with you forever—the Spirit of truth. The world cannot accept him, because it neither sees him nor knows him. But you know him, for he lives with you and will be in you. I will not leave you as orphans; I will come to you. Before long, the world will not see me anymore, but you will see me. Because I live, you also will live. On that day you will realize that I am in my Father, and you are in me, and I am in you." (John 14:16-20)

"All this I have spoken while still with you. But the Counselor, the Holy Spirit, whom the Father will send in my name, will teach you all things and will remind you of everything I have said to you." (John 14:25-26)

"But I tell you the truth: It is for your good that I am going away. Unless I go away, the Counselor will not come to you; but if I go, I will send him to you. When he comes, he will convict the world of guilt in regard to sin and righteousness and judgment: in regard to sin, because men do not believe in me; in regard to righteousness, because I am going to the Father, where you can see me no longer; and in regard to judgment, because the prince of this world now stands condemned.

"I have much more to say to you, more than you can

*now bear. But when he, the Spirit of truth, comes, he will
guide you into all truth. He will not speak on his own; he
will speak only what he hears, and he will tell you what is
yet to come. He will bring glory to me by taking from what
is mine and making it known to you. All that belongs to
the Father is mine. That is why I said the Spirit will take
from what is mine and make it known to you." (John 16:7-15)*

It is perhaps significant that so much of Jesus' teaching regarding the Holy Spirit occurs at this time. It was
customary in the Old Testament for there to be a dynas-
tic succession celebration at the time of covenant re-
newals. For example, we look to the record of the end
of Moses' life when he gives a charge to the people and
to his successor Joshua:

*Then Moses went out and spoke these words to all Israel: "I
am now a hundred and twenty years old and I am no longer
able to lead you. The LORD has said to me, 'You shall not
cross the Jordan.' The LORD your God himself will cross
over ahead of you. He will destroy these nations before you,
and you will take possession of their land. Joshua also will
cross over ahead of you, as the LORD said. And the LORD
will do to them what he did to Sihon and Og, the kings of
the Amorites, whom he destroyed along with their land.
The LORD will deliver them to you, and you must do to
them all that I have commanded you. Be strong and
courageous. Do not be afraid or terrified because of them,
for the LORD your God goes with you; he will never leave
you nor forsake you."*

*Then Moses summoned Joshua and said to him in the
presence of all Israel, "Be strong and courageous, for you
must go with this people into the land that the LORD swore
to their forefathers to give them, and you must divide it
among them as their inheritance. The LORD himself goes*

before you and will be with you; he will never leave you nor forsake you. Do not be afraid; do not be discouraged." (Deuteronomy 31:1-8)

On this occasion the covenant was renewed and the leadership passed from Moses to Joshua. In the upper room Jesus announces His departure and promises the abiding presence of the Holy Spirit in their midst. The mediator of the New Covenant on the occasion of His imminent departure is concerned that His people not be left as orphans.

John also records the lengthy "high priestly prayer" of Jesus. At the heart of this prayer is the subject of glorification. Jesus' "hour" has finally come upon Him, and it becomes the focal point of His prayer:

After Jesus said this, he looked toward heaven and prayed: "Father, the time has come. Glorify your Son, that your Son may glorify you. For you granted him authority over all people that he might give eternal life to all those you have given him. Now this is eternal life: that they may know you, the only true God, and Jesus Christ, whom you have sent. I have brought you glory on earth by completing the work you gave me to do. And now, Father, glorify me in your presence with the glory I had with you before the world began. (John 17:1-5)

Jesus' prayer concerns a matter of reciprocal glory. He directly asks the Father to glorify the Son. The purpose of this request, however, is not one that is self-seeking. The purpose for the request is clear: that the Son may also glorify the Father.

At the time of the Protestant Reformation, one of the key slogans that was used was *Soli Deo Gloria*—"To

God alone be the glory." It is because Jesus Himself is God incarnate that it is proper for Him to participate in the glory of the Godhead. Glory belongs to Jesus. In His prayer in the upper room He is not asking for something that is not properly His. Jesus declares that He has glorified the Father during His own earthly ministry and now asks that He may be glorified together with the Father. He asks to receive the glory that He had with the Father before the creation of the world.

Jesus is therefore not asking for something new to be added to Him. He asks for the restoration of what was His from all eternity. That eternal glory had been masked, voluntarily hidden from public view during His incarnation. His messianic task is about to be completed. He looks beyond the shadow of the cross that looms before Him to the return to the realm of glory from which He came.

Jesus not only prays for the restoration of His own glory; He prays that those who belong to Him may share in the presence of His glory. Jesus not only prayed for His disciples who walked with Him on earth but for us and all who embrace Him through the testimony of the apostles:

"My prayer is not for them alone. I pray also for those who will believe in me through their message, that all of them may be one, Father, just as you are in me and I am in you. May they also be in us so that the world may believe that you have sent me. I have given them the glory that you gave me, that they may be one as we are one: I in them and you in me. May they be brought to complete unity to let the

*world know that you sent me and have loved them even as
you have loved me.*

*"Father, I want those you have given me to be with me
where I am, and to see my glory, the glory you have given
me because you loved me before the creation of the world."*
(John 17:20-24)

Shortly after this prayer Jesus will pray another one.
He will enter into the agony of His passion in Gethsemane. But before He enters into that prayer struggle, He
devotes His prayer to one of intercession for us. He asks
the Father that we may enter into His presence and
behold His glory.

The church has every reason to be confident that the
prayer Jesus made in our behalf will be fulfilled. Later
John proclaimed the surety of the beatific vision that
every believer will enjoy:

*How great is the love the Father has lavished on us, that
we should be called children of God! And that is what we
are! The reason the world does not know us is that it did
not know him. Dear friends, now we are children of God,
and what we will be has not yet been made known. But we
know that when he appears, we shall be like him, for we
shall see him as he is. Everyone who has this hope in him
purifies himself, just as he is pure.* (1 John 3:1-3)

CHAPTER TWELVE

GLORY ON THE CROSS

In the cross of Christ I glory,
Towering o'er the wrecks of time;
All the light of sacred story
Gathers round its head sublime.

JOHN BOWRING

W

E LIVE IN a topsy-turvy world. The riches of God are considered trash by men. What God esteems we despise, and what is enticing to us is repugnant to Him. To search for glory in the cross of Christ is to turn the values of man upside down. Yet in this darkest hour of human history we see light piercing the shadows, a beam that beckons us to look beyond the obvious, to peer above the shadow to the glory beyond. Without light there can be no shadow.

At the same time, but by no means in the same relationship, the cross stands as the nadir of history and the zenith of divine glory. It is tragedy and victory in the same moment. It is scandal and honor, defeat and triumph, shame and esteem. Paul understood the irony of the cross: "May I never boast except in the cross of our Lord Jesus Christ, through which the world has been crucified to me, and I to the world" (Galatians 6:14). Where some translations use the word *boast*, other translations use *glory*. Paul glories in the cross. It is, for him, an occasion of boasting, something to be proud of. In the cross Paul sees not only the crucifixion of Christ but also the crucifixion of himself and of the world.

The cross represents the *passio magnum*, the great suffering of Christ. The suffering far transcends physical pain. It is more than a human death; it is an atonement. Christ is the sacrificial lamb. He must bear the weight of divine displeasure. He must feel the wrath of the Father poured out against sin. He must not only be executed by man, He must be forsaken by God.

In the events surrounding Jesus' death there are tiny rays of glory that seep through the cloud cover of humiliation. We see a few of these in the record of His trial. After His betrayal with a kiss by Judas, Jesus was arrested in the Garden of Gethsemane on the slopes of the Mount of Olives. The arresting officers took Him first to Annas, the father-in-law of Caiaphas the high priest, and then to Caiaphas himself. John notes that it was Caiaphas who gave counsel to the Sanhedrin that it was "expedient that one man should die for the people" (John 18:14).

Caiaphas' judgment had been rendered strictly for political expediency. He feared reprisals from Rome if Jesus' popularity increased. He showed no concern for real justice. He was willing to sacrifice an innocent man for the sake of maintaining political stability. He was weighing the "greatest good for the greatest number" without regard for individual justice.

In his crass political judgment, Caiaphas uttered words that were far more prophetic than he could imagine. Caiaphas obviously had no idea how expedient it was for the nation that Jesus be put to death. He could not see beyond his own and his nation's political interests. Yet out of his mouth came an evaluation that had cosmic relevance. The good inherent in the execution of Jesus was not that it might pacify a potentially angry Roman emperor but in its satisfaction of the just wrath of an angry God. No more expedient sacrifice

was ever offered for any people than the sacrifice offered by Christ in His death.

The death of Christ was both a *propitiation* and an
expiation of sin. Propitiation refers to the turning away
of wrath by an offering. God's wrath is satisfied, His
justice is met by the sacrifice. Expiation refers to cover-
ing sins. By the atonement our sins are removed from
us. The atonement satisfies both the demands of the
Father and the needs of Christ's people. That such a
double transaction can be achieved by one Person in
one event is a matter of eternal glory.

THE TESTIMONY OF PILATE

Caiaphas was not the only player in the drama of
Jesus' trial who spoke words far more pregnant than the
speaker realized. The Roman governor Pilate also uttered wisdom beyond his means as his simple words
bore.

During the interrogation, Pilate declared Jesus' innocence three times:

*"What is truth?" Pilate asked. With this he went out
again to the Jews and said, "I find no basis for a charge
against him."* (John 18:38)

*Once more Pilate came out and said to the Jews, "Look, I
am bringing him out to you to let you know that I find no
basis for a charge against him."* (John 19:4)

*As soon as the chief priests and their officials saw him, they
shouted, "Crucify! Crucify!" But Pilate answered, "You
take him and crucify him. As for me, I find no basis for a
charge against him."* (John 19:6)

151

Other translations render Pilate's words "I find no fault in Him." Three times Pilate indicated that his investigation rendered no basis for charging Jesus with anything. He was unable to find fault with Him.

Pilate was a *persona publica*, a duly appointed earthly magistrate. His role in God's plan of redemption is noted in the Apostle's Creed. Pilate was unaware that this episode in his tenure as procurator of a small province in the Roman Empire would secure him a place in world history.

His words, "I find no fault in Him," go deeper than their surface meaning. Pilate could find no fault because there was no fault. This was the only time in history that a civil magistrate was asked to pass judgment on a sinless human being.

Understanding the faultlessness of Jesus is central to our understanding of the cross. For an atonement to be acceptable to God, it was necessary that the sacrificial lamb had to be without blemish. The utter sinlessness of Jesus qualified Him to be our Savior. The death of a man was not sufficient to pay the penalty prescribed by the law of God. It had to be a *sinless* man. Had Jesus' character been marred by a single transgression, He would not have qualified to save us by His death.

It is the life of Christ that is as crucial for our redemption as His death. God did not simply send His incarnate Son immediately from heaven, full grown, and execute Him on the spot at the moment of His arrival. Before Christ could die for us He had to first live for us. As the new Adam, He had to pass the test of the Law. His life of perfect obedience was a necessary prerequisite for His perfect sacrifice.

It is the achievement of perfect obedience that is indirectly and cryptically attested by Pilate's verdict. Thus his words, "I find no fault in Him," take on transcendent meaning.

Pilate's unwitting testimony reaches another dimension when he makes another now famous declaration: "When Jesus came out wearing the crown of thorns and the purple robe, Pilate said to them, 'Here is the man!'" (John 19:5). Some translations have, "Behold the man!" This phrase has made its way into the theological tradition of the church through its Latin form, *Ecce homo*. On Pilate's lips it sounds like a statement of mockery as Jesus was presented in the mock uniform of a king. To behold the man in the deepest sense of the phrase is precisely what Pilate and those with him failed to do. Their gaze was superficial. If they had beheld the depths of the man standing before them, they would have seen the embodiment of a new humanity. Pilate was looking at the perfect man, but his eyes were blind to it.

There is another hint of the glory of Christ that escapes during the interrogation. When Pilate grew afraid he questioned Jesus further:

When Pilate heard this, he was even more afraid, and he went back inside the palace. "Where do you come from?" he asked Jesus, but Jesus gave him no answer. "Do you refuse to speak to me?" Pilate said. "Don't you realize I have power either to free you or to crucify you?"

Jesus answered, "You would have no power over me if it

153

were not given to you from above. Therefore the one who handed me over to you is guilty of a greater sin." (John 19:8-11)

Here Pilate tries to intimidate Jesus. He says to Him, "Don't you realize I have power either to free you or to crucify you?" Obviously the true answer to Pilate's question was "No!" Pilate had never met a prisoner who was less able to be intimidated than Jesus. The fearlessness of Jesus was disconcerting. Pilate assumed that such fearlessness must be rooted in the prisoner's ignorance. It must be, he thought, that Jesus simply did not realize who He was dealing with. The reverse was the case. Pilate did not realize whom he was dealing with.

Jesus replied by correcting Pilate's false assumptions: He explained to Pilate that he had no power, no authority except what was given from above. Power and authority are granted by God.

This reply of Jesus is filled with meaning. It is central to the New Testament portrait of Jesus that His death was *voluntary*. It was a work of active obedience to the Father, not passive obedience. There was no conflict between the will of the Father and the will of the Son. It was His voluntary decision to lay down His life for His sheep. He made that clear in the Good Shepherd discourse:

"I am the good shepherd; I know my sheep and my sheep know me—just as the Father knows me and I know the Father—and I lay down my life for the sheep. I have other sheep that are not of this sheep pen. I must bring them also. They too will listen to my voice, and there shall be one flock

154

*and one shepherd. The reason my Father loves me is that
I lay down my life—only to take it up again. No one
takes it from me, but I lay it down of my own accord. I
have authority to lay it down and authority to take it up
again. This command I received from my Father."* (John
10:14-18)

Pilate unwittingly made one more statement that exceeded in truth his own intent:

*Pilate had a notice prepared and fastened to the cross. It
read: JESUS OF NAZARETH, THE KING OF THE JEWS.
Many of the Jews read this sign, for the place where Jesus
was crucified was near the city, and the sign was written
in Aramaic, Latin, and Greek. The chief priests of the
Jews protested to Pilate, "Do not write 'The King of the
Jews,' but that this man claimed to be king of the Jews."*

Pilate answered, "What I have written, I have written."
(John 19:19-22)

The Jewish authorities protested Pilate's designation
of Jesus as the king of the Jews. Pilate refused to erase
it. Probably he was protecting his own action in light
of his personal accountability to Roman law. The only
legal justification Pilate had was to execute Jesus on
the grounds of sedition for claiming royal authority.
His terse response to the demands was "What I have
written, I have written." What he wrote was, in reality,
the sober truth. Jesus was the king of the Jews, the
Messiah God had promised His people.

Much attention has been given to the details of the
crucifixion of Jesus. As ghastly as the pain of crucifixion
was, we know that multitudes of persons went through
such affliction. But no human being, before or since,

was ever called upon to endure the affliction that was heaped upon Jesus. By comparison with the pain inflicted by divine wrath and judgment of the paschal lamb, the physical pain was nothing.

The cry Jesus uttered from the cross did not directly complain of the pain. His lament focused upon forsakenness:

From the sixth hour until the ninth hour darkness came over all the land. About the ninth hour Jesus cried out in a loud voice, "Eloi, Eloi, lama sabachthani?"—which means, "My God, my God, why have you forsaken me?" (Matthew 27:45-46)

This lament is surely the most anguishing cry ever to escape from the lips of Jesus. The anguished words are from Psalm 22, a passage that has many interesting parallels with the crucifixion.

My God, my God, why have you forsaken me?
 Why are you so far from saving me,
 so far from the words of my groaning?
O my God, I cry out by day, but you do not answer,
 by night, and am not silent.
Yet you are enthroned as the Holy One;
 you are the praise of Israel.
In you our fathers put their trust;
 they trusted and you delivered them.
They cried to you and were saved;
 in you they trusted and were not disappointed.
But I am a worm and not a man,
 scorned by men and despised by the people.
All who see me mock me;
 they hurl insults, shaking their heads:
"He trusts in the LORD;
 let the LORD rescue him.

Let him deliver him,
  since he delights in him."
Yet you brought me out of the womb;
  you made me trust in you
  even at my mother's breast.
From birth I was cast upon you;
  from my mother's womb you have been my God.
Do not be far from me,
  for trouble is near
  and there is no one to help.
Many bulls surround me;
  strong bulls of Bashan encircle me.
Roaring lions tearing their prey
  open their mouths wide against me.
I am poured out like water,
  and all my bones are out of joint.
My heart has turned to wax;
  it has melted away within me.
My strength is dried up like a potsherd,
  and my tongue sticks to the roof of my mouth;
  you lay me in the dust of death.
Dogs have surrounded me;
  a band of evil men has encircled me,
  they have pierced my hands and my feet.
I can count all my bones;
  people stare and gloat over me.
They divide my garments among them
  and cast lots for my clothing.

(Psalm 22:1-18)

This sounds like an eyewitness report of the crucifixion of Jesus, even down to the details of the casting of lots for His garments. But the chief interest in the Psalm concerns the opening line, "My God, my God, why have you forsaken me?" Did Jesus cite this Psalm

157

merely to show that He was fulfilling prophecy? Surely
He was familiar with the Psalm and used its words
to express His agony. But it is virtually certain that
Jesus was doing more than merely quoting Scripture to
provide a Bible lesson for the spectators. By identifying with the words of this Psalm, He was giving expression to the reality of the forsakenness He was
experiencing.

One of my favorite hymns, the hymn I chose for
my ordination service, is the Communion hymn, "'Tis
Midnight and on Olive's Brow." Much as I love the
hymn, I find fault with the verse that declares, "Was not
forsaken by His God." We must not think that Jesus
merely *felt* forsaken on the cross but in reality was not
forsaken. On the contrary, the very essence of the cross
was the utter forsakenness of Christ.

To be forsaken by God is the ultimate penalty for sin.
The pit of hell is the abode of the utterly forsaken. To
be forsaken is to be cast into the outer darkness. It is to
receive the fury of the curse of God.

We have already seen the terms of the covenant that
God made with His people. That covenant had two
sanctions; the promise of blessedness for those who
obey the stipulations of the covenant and the threat of
the curse for those who disobey. To the Jew, to be cursed
of God is to be cut off from the light of His presence.
In the Old Testament rite of atonement the scapegoat
is loaded down by the transfer of the people's sins to its
back. It is then driven outside the camp, outside the
scope of the presence of God, to be abandoned to the

wilderness. Removal from the divine presence is the fate of the scapegoat and of all who are accursed by God.

Paul develops this idea in his Letter to the Galatians:

All who rely on observing the law are under a curse, for it is written: "Cursed is everyone who does not continue to do everything written in the Book of the Law." Clearly no one is justified before God by the law, because, "The righteous will live by faith." The law is not based on faith; on the contrary, "The man who does these things will live by them." Christ redeemed us from the curse of the law by becoming a curse for us, for it is written: "Cursed is everyone who is hung on a tree." (Galatians 3:10-13)

On the cross Jesus does not merely receive the curse of God, He becomes the curse. He is the embodiment of the curse. Every aspect of cursing converges upon Jesus in His trial and death. His judgment and sentence came from Romans after the Jews had sent Him "outside the camp." He died by crucifixion, the Roman method of execution. Had He been executed under Jewish law He would have been stoned. As Paul indicates, citing Deuteronomy, bodies that hung upon trees were considered defiled and accursed. The means of Jesus' death was therefore accursed under Jewish Law.

The site of Jesus' execution was also significant. The crucifixion did not take place within the Holy City of Jerusalem. Golgotha was outside the city gates. Here Jesus the scapegoat was cut off from His people, His city, and His God.

The prophet Habakkuk declared:

Your eyes are too pure to look on evil;
  you cannot tolerate wrong.

Why then do you tolerate the treacherous?
  Why are you silent while the wicked
  swallow up those more righteous than themselves?
                                        (Habakkuk 1:13)

God is so holy that He cannot gaze upon sin. It is repugnant to His eyes. Before Jesus ascends to the cross He is altogether lovely in the sight of the Father. He is the brightness of the Father's glory and the express image of His person. As such Christ is, in the eyes of the Father, a thing of unspeakable beauty. He is the Father's beloved.

Once Jesus willingly assumes the burden of the sin of His people, everything changes. When the sin of man is transferred to Him as the sins of Israel were transferred to the scapegoat, what once was delightful to the Father becomes odious to Him. On the cross Jesus becomes in the sight of God the most grotesque display of ugliness imaginable. He is now polluted with the cumulative filth of the sin He bears for His sheep. Now the Father breaks fellowship with Him; He averts His divine glance; Jesus as the very incarnation of sin is consigned to the outer darkness.

While Jesus hung on the cross there was a noted cosmic disturbance. "From the sixth hour until the ninth hour darkness came over all the land" (Matthew 27:45). Though the execution of Jesus took place in midafternoon, the day became as night. It is as if God not only turned the light of His countenance off Jesus, but He turned out the lights for planet earth. At this moment there is no glory. The radiance is quenched. All that is left is the curse of forsakenness.

Where is the glory in that? For Jesus in that moment there certainly was none. But for us it was the greatest moment in world history. At one and the same time the moment in time that held the fullest expression of divine wrath and judgment was the moment of the greatest expression of His glorious grace. The justice of the event is seen in that sin was not winked at but truly and fully punished. The grace is seen in that the punishment was borne by a substitute provided by God Himself.

John Calvin once struggled with the Apostle's Creed's phrase "He descended into hell." He did not quarrel with the accuracy of the phrase but with its place in the structure of the creed. Calvin wished to change the order in this manner: The traditional structure reads: "Suffered under Pontius Pilate; crucified, dead, and buried. He descended into hell." Calvin preferred to reorder the lines so they would read like this: "Suffered under Pontius Pilate; was crucified, descended into hell, dead, and buried." Calvin rightly understood that Jesus received the punishment of hell while He was on the cross.

There came a moment when the curse was lifted and the forsakenness was complete. Jesus cried out, "It is finished!" (John 19:30). The Greek word John's Gospel has is *tetelestai*. It was used in the world of commerce to signify the final payment has been made—that is, the account is "Paid in full." The price for the purchase of our souls had been fully remitted, and Jesus cried in relief that it was over.

Jesus' words from the cross recorded by Luke are important: "Jesus called out with a loud voice, 'Father, into your hands I commit my spirit.' When he had said this, he breathed his last" (Luke 23:46). This final cry indicates that the curse has been removed. Fellowship with the Father has been restored.

The witnessing of this spectacle provoked a Roman centurion to glorify God: "And when the centurion, who stood there in front of Jesus, heard his cry and saw how he died, he said, 'Surely this man was the Son of God!'" (Mark 15:39).

There are other details about the crucifixion that indicate breakthroughs of glory in this darkest hour of Jesus' life. Mark tells us that at the moment of Jesus' death the veil of the temple was torn in two from top to bottom. Apart from its theological significance, the fact itself is remarkable. The veil of the temple was the "wall of partition" that separated the Holy Place from the Holy of Holies. It is described in the Book of Exodus:

Make a curtain of blue, purple and scarlet yarn and finely twisted linen, with cherubim worked into it by a skilled craftsman. Hang it with gold hooks on four posts of acacia wood overlaid with gold and standing on four silver bases. Hang the curtain from the clasps and place the ark of the Testimony behind the curtain. The curtain will separate the Holy Place from the Most Holy Place. (Exodus 26:31-33)

The curtain was not a single sheet of cloth that could easily be ripped in two from top to bottom. It was multilayered, and no hands were strong enough or big enough to even begin to rip such a veil in two. It was an act of God. God rips the wall of partition because of the acceptability to Him of the atonement that was made by Christ. Where once sinful man was barred from His presence, access was now possible because of the cross. Paul viewed this as one of the primary fruits of justification that is afforded all who place their faith in the work of Christ:

Since we have been justified through faith, we have peace with God through our Lord Jesus Christ, through whom we have gained access by faith into this grace in which we now stand. And we rejoice in the hope of the glory of God. (Romans 5:1-2)

Matthew provides another mysterious, though glorious, detail that accompanied the crucifixion of Christ:

At that moment the curtain of the temple was torn in two from top to bottom. The earth shook and the rocks split. The tombs broke open and the bodies of many holy people who had died were raised to life. They came out of the tombs, and after Jesus' resurrection they went into the holy city and appeared to many people. (Matthew 27:51-53)

Here Matthew records a cataclysmic event that accompanied the cross. An earthquake shook Jerusalem, disturbing the tombs of the saints.

For those who walked out of their graves, this day of infamy was a day of glory, even as it was for all who embrace the perfect sacrifice of Christ. Christ's hour had come. Now the progress of His glorification was at hand.

CHAPTER THIRTEEN

GLORY
IN THE
RESURRECTION

Jesus Christ was born twice.
The birth at Bethlehem was a birth
into a life of weakness.
The second time he was born from the grave—
"the first-born from the dead"—
into the glory of heaven and the throne of God.

ANDREW MURRAY

O N THE CROSS Jesus reached the lowest point of His humiliation. The question is often posed, At what specific point does the transition occur from humiliation to exaltation? The frequent answer we hear to this question is the Resurrection. However, there is a point prior to the Resurrection that the transition is actually made.

THE BURIAL OF JESUS

The circumstances of Jesus' burial point to a transition from humiliation to exaltation. Normally the corpses of executed criminals were either left on the cross to be devoured by vultures or thrown unceremoniously into Gehenna, the garbage dump outside Jerusalem. Gehenna served as an apt symbol for hell among the Jews because it was a place of perpetual fire. The refuse that was regularly added to the dump was continuously being disposed of by burning. At all times the dump was at least smoldering. Intercession was made for the body of Jesus that it might not be shown the indignity of being thrown on the refuse heap:

Joseph of Arimathea asked Pilate for the body of Jesus. Now Joseph was a disciple of Jesus, but secretly because he feared the Jews. With Pilate's permission, he came and took the body away. He was accompanied by Nicodemus, the man who earlier had visited Jesus at night. Nicodemus brought a mixture of myrrh and aloes, about seventy-five pounds. Taking Jesus' body, the two of them wrapped it, with the spices, in strips of linen. This was in accordance with Jewish burial customs. At the place where Jesus was crucified, there was a garden, and in the garden a new tomb, in which no one had ever been laid. Because it was the Jewish day of Preparation and since the tomb was nearby, they laid Jesus there. (John 19:38-42)

The amount of spices Nicodemus brought for the anointing of Jesus' body was extravagant. It was befitting of a royal burial. This action, taken together with the quality of the grave site itself, calls attention to the fulfillment of the prophecy of Isaiah:

By oppression and judgment he was taken away.
And who can speak of his descendants?
For he was cut off from the land of the living;
for the transgression of my people he was stricken.
He was assigned a grave with the wicked,
and with the rich in his death,
though he had done no violence,
nor was any deceit in his mouth.

(Isaiah 53:8-9)

The force of this text is that the Suffering Servant of Israel would die in the company of the wicked, but because of His innocence His grave would be with the rich. The richness of Jesus' burial marks a clear transition from humiliation to exaltation. Both Peter on the Day of Pentecost and Paul in a sermon at Antioch made reference to the Old Testament promise that God would not allow His Holy One to see corruption:

The fact that God raised him from the dead, never to decay, is stated in these words:

"I will give you the holy and sure blessings promised to David."

So it is stated elsewhere:

"You will not let your Holy One see decay."

For when David had served God's purpose in his own generation, he fell asleep; he was buried with his fathers and his body decayed. But the one whom God raised from the dead did not see decay. (Acts 13:34-37)

EASTER MORNING

The Gospels tell us that it was Mary Magdalene who first approached the site of Jesus' tomb on Sunday morning. She was accompanied by the "other" Mary. They were startled and confused to see the huge sealing stone rolled away. Matthew gives this account:

After the Sabbath, at dawn on the first day of the week, Mary Magdalene and the other Mary went to look at the tomb.

There was a violent earthquake, for an angel of the Lord came down from heaven and, going to the tomb, rolled back the stone and sat on it. His appearance was like lightning, and his clothes were white as snow. The guards were so afraid of him that they shook and became like dead men.

The angel said to the women, "Do not be afraid, for I know that you are looking for Jesus, who was crucified. He is not here; he has risen, just as he said. Come and see the place where he lay. Then go quickly and tell his disciples: 'He has risen from the dead and is going ahead of you into Galilee. There you will see him.' Now I have told you."

So the women hurried away from the tomb, afraid yet filled with joy, and ran to tell his disciples. (Matthew 28:1-8)

169

Luke adds the detail that there were two angels or "men in shining garments" that announced the Resurrection to the women. The visible appearance of the angels indicates the presence of glory that surrounded the empty tomb. As is usually the case with the appearance of angels in glory those who behold them are stricken with terror. The task of the guards of the tomb was an exercise in futility. They had no power to prevent the invasion of the burial place by the angelic visitors. They became as dead men, paralyzed in fear.

The women returned to report their findings to the disciples. Peter and John raced to the site to investigate. John reports what they discovered:

He bent over and looked in at the strips of linen lying there but did not go in. Then Simon Peter, who was behind him, arrived and went into the tomb. He saw the strips of linen lying there, as well as the burial cloth that had been around Jesus' head. The cloth was folded up by itself, separate from the linen. Finally the other disciple, who had reached the tomb first, also went inside. He saw and believed. (John 20:5-8)

The details supplied concerning the graveclothes had significance in the early church. The enemies of Jesus contended that the disciples had stolen the body of Christ. They left unexplained how they managed to get past the guards and move the stone. Moreover, it would be unnecessary and undesirable for thieves to first strip the body of Jesus and then take the time to fold the handkerchief that covered His head.

THE APPEARANCE OF THE RISEN CHRIST

After Peter and John discovered the empty tomb and the graveclothes in place, they returned to their homes. Mary Magdalene tarried by the tomb:

But Mary stood outside the tomb crying. As she wept, she bent over to look into the tomb and saw two angels in white, seated where Jesus' body had been, one at the head and the other at the foot.

They asked her, "Woman, why are you crying?"

"They have taken my Lord away," she said, "and I don't know where they have put him." At this, she turned around and saw Jesus standing there, but she did not realize that it was Jesus.

"Woman," he said, "why are you crying? Who is it you are looking for?"

Thinking he was the gardener, she said, "Sir, if you have carried him away, tell me where you have put him, and I will get him."

Jesus said to her, "Mary."

She turned toward him and cried out in Aramaic, "Rabboni!" (which means Teacher).

Jesus said, "Do not hold on to me, for I have not yet returned to the Father. Go instead to my brothers and tell them, 'I am returning to my Father and your Father, to my God and your God.'"

Mary Magdalene went to the disciples with the news: "I have seen the Lord!" And she told them that he had said these things to her. (John 20:11-18)

Mary was obviously in a state of shock. She had been excited by the first sight of the tomb and the message of the angels. Now she gives way to tears of fear and frustration. She expressed her fears that someone had taken away the body of Jesus. She turned away from the tomb and saw a man standing whom she supposed to be the gardener. Jesus addressed her tenderly and asked why she was crying. Again she expressed her fear that the body of Jesus had been taken away. Then Jesus called her by name. There was instant recognition of the voice. Why Jesus was not first recognizable to her may be explained partly by here distressed emotional state (it is difficult to see clearly through tears) and partly by the transformation of Jesus' body into a glorified state. Yet when she heard Him utter her name there was instant recognition.

THE ROAD TO EMMAUS

On the day of the Resurrection, two of the company of Jesus' followers were traveling to the village of Emmaus, about seven miles from Jerusalem. They were discussing the events in Jerusalem. As they talked, Jesus drew near to them. The Bible says that their eyes were restrained in such a way that they were unable to recognize Him. Jesus asked them why they were so sad and what it was they were discussing. Cleopas was obviously annoyed by the apparent impertinence of the question. He said to Jesus, "Are you only a visitor to Jerusalem and do not know the things that have happened there in these days?"(Luke 24:18). Jesus answered Cleopas's question as if He were indeed a stranger to the things that had happened in Jerusalem. He said to him, "What things?" (Luke 24:19).

In their explanation, the two men revealed their struggle to believe the reports they had heard:

But we had hoped that he was the one who was going to redeem Israel. And what is more, it is the third day since all this took place. In addition, some of our women amazed us. They went to the tomb early this morning but didn't find his body. They came and told us that they had seen a vision of angels, who said he was alive. Then some of our companions went to the tomb and found it just as the women had said, but him they did not see. (Luke 24:21-24)

We notice that Cleopas spoke of the hope they had in Jesus in the past tense. He referred to the experience of the women who had seen the angels as a "vision." Then he reported the findings of the disciples who had visited the empty tomb but was quick to point out that they had not actually seen the risen Jesus. So far all they had was the testimony of women and the verification of the empty tomb. The empty tomb in itself did not prove the Resurrection.

After Jesus patiently listened to their account, He responded to it with a sharp rebuke:

He said to them, "How foolish you are, and how slow of heart to believe all that the prophets have spoken! Did not the Christ have to suffer these things and then enter his glory?" And beginning with Moses and all the Prophets, he explained to them what was said in all the Scriptures concerning himself. (Luke 24:25-27)

Jesus rebuked them for their slowness of faith. They were not prepared to believe until they had seen Him with their own eyes. It is significant that Jesus did not choose to open their eyes at that precise instant to give them the eyewitness proof they wanted. Instead He instructed them from the Old Testament Scriptures, which should have been testimony enough had they been diligent students of the Word of God.

It was not until they entered their quarters in Emmaus and sat at the table to break bread that their eyes were opened to recognize Jesus. Luke describes the moment:

When he was at the table with them, he took bread, gave thanks, broke it and began to give it to them. Then their eyes were opened and they recognized him, and he disappeared from their sight. They asked each other, "Were not our hearts burning within us while he talked with us on the road and opened the Scriptures to us?" (Luke 24:30-32)

Now their encounter with the stranger made sense to them. As Jesus vanished from their presence, they were left startled and amazed. They recalled the sensations they experienced when they had listened to Jesus teach them from the Old Testament on the road.

THE CONFESSION OF THOMAS

On the evening of the same day Jesus appeared to the men on the road to Emmaus, He appeared to His disciples in the upper room:

On the evening of that first day of the week, when the disciples were together, with the doors locked for fear of the Jews, Jesus came and stood among them and said, "Peace be with you!" (John 20:19)

The door was locked. The passage seems to suggest that Jesus suddenly appeared in the room without having entered through an open door. Doctoral dissertations have been written about the nature of Christ's risen body, arguing that in its glorified state it had the ability to pass unimpeded through solid objects and to move large distances in an instant. He "vanished" suddenly from the meal with the men in Emmaus and now, just as suddenly, appears in the room where the door was locked. The Bible does not explicitly say that Jesus walked *through* the locked door or that His body had the ability to materialize suddenly from place to place. It is possible that John mentions the detail of the locked door not to indicate anything about the nature of Jesus' glorified body but to indicate something about the emotional state of the disciples. He gives the reason for the locked door; it was "for fear of the Jews." The disciples were in hiding. They huddled in fear that they would be arrested for being accomplices of Jesus. Perhaps what is left unstated is that while they were cringing in fear there was a knock at the door and Jesus was then admitted to their presence. That is a possible interpretation, but the probable sense of the verse is that Jesus did in fact appear in their midst without the benefit of having the door opened for Him.

Luke's account of the appearance in their midst adds another significant detail:

While they were still talking about this, Jesus himself stood among them and said to them, "Peace be with you."
They were startled and frightened, thinking they saw a ghost. (Luke 24:36-37)

If we add together all the references to Jesus' Resurrection appearances, including the fact that He was difficult to recognize by Mary Magdalene and the men in Emmaus, it seems likely that Jesus' glorified body was significantly different from His earlier body. Something was obviously different about Him. At the same time, there was also continuity. The disciples were able to identify Him positively. He was not a ghost. He had a real body. His body that was buried was not destroyed or left behind. But that body was changed. The changes in it are hinted at by Paul's description of the nature of a glorified body:

But someone may ask, "How are the dead raised? With what kind of body will they come?" How foolish! What you sow does not come to life unless it dies. When you sow, you do not plant the body that will be, but just a seed, perhaps of wheat or of something else. But God gives it a body as he has determined, and to each kind of seed he gives its own body. All flesh is not the same: Men have one kind of flesh, animals have another, birds another and fish another. There are also heavenly bodies and there are earthly bodies; but the splendor of the heavenly bodies is one kind, and the splendor of the earthly bodies is another. The sun has one kind of splendor, the moon another and the stars another; and star differs from star in splendor.

So will it be with the Resurrection of the dead. The body that is sown is perishable, it is raised imperishable; it is sown in dishonor, it is raised in glory; it is sown in weakness, it is raised in power; it is sown a natural body, it is raised a spiritual body.

If there is a natural body, there is also a spiritual body.
(1 Corinthians 15:35-44)

In this passage Paul provides valuable information concerning what we can expect will happen to us in the raising of our bodies. The distinction he makes is between a "natural" body and a "spiritual" body. "Spiritual body" sounds like a contradiction in terms to us. We think of spirit and body as mutually exclusive. This is not the Hebrew sense, however. Angelic beings are spirits, but they have a definite finite form. They are not infinite spirits. A spiritual body is localized. It is contained to a definite space. It may be less solid and more vaporous in its composition, but it is still a form of matter. What Paul describes as the nature of spiritual body he grounds in the power and example of the risen Christ:

So it is written: "The first man Adam became a living being"; the last Adam, a life-giving spirit. The spiritual did not come first, but the natural, and after that the spiritual. The first man was of the dust of the earth, the second man from heaven. As was the earthly man, so are those who are of the earth; and as is the man from heaven, so also are those who are of heaven. And just as we have borne the likeness of the earthly man, so shall we bear the likeness of the man from heaven.

I declare to you, brothers, that flesh and blood cannot inherit the kingdom of God, nor does the perishable inherit the imperishable. Listen, I tell you a mystery: We will not all sleep, but we will all be changed—in a flash, in the twinkling of an eye, at the last trumpet. For the trumpet will sound, the dead will be raised imperishable, and we will be changed. For the perishable must clothe itself with the imperishable, and the mortal with immortality. When the perishable has been clothed with the imperishable, and the mortal with immortality, then the saying that is written will come true: "Death has been swallowed up in victory." (1 Corinthians 15:45-54)

This passage sheds light on the nature of Jesus' risen body. The body was still material, as seen in the manifestation of its parts that Jesus displayed to His disciples: "After he said this, he showed them his hands and side. The disciples were overjoyed when they saw the Lord" (John 20:20). Luke adds further details:

He said to them, "Why are you troubled, and why do doubts rise in your minds? Look at my hands and my feet. It is I myself! Touch me and see; a ghost does not have flesh and bones, as you see I have."

When he had said this, he showed them his hands and feet. And while they still did not believe it because of joy and amazement, he asked them, "Do you have anything here to eat?" They gave him a piece of broiled fish, and he took it and ate it in their presence. (Luke 24:38-43)

It is clear that though Jesus' body has become a spiritual body, it is a real body. He still has some sort of flesh and bones. He was still capable of eating.

For some reason Thomas was absent from the group. When the other disciples reported Jesus' appearance to him, he was skeptical:

Now Thomas (called Didymus), one of the Twelve, was not with the disciples when Jesus came. So the other disciples told him, "We have seen the Lord!"

But he said to them, "Unless I see the nail marks in his hands and put my finger where the nails were, and put my hand into his side, I will not believe it." (John 20:24-25)

Thomas was unwilling to believe the Resurrection simply on the basis of the disciples' testimony. Despite the fact that they were in agreement about what happened, Thomas demanded more evidence. He insisted that he must see with his eyes and touch with his own hands before he would accept the Resurrection.

The empirical verification he demanded was, indeed, given to him, but not without an eight-day interlude. One wonders how many arguments the disciples had with Thomas during that time. Surely each day that passed without further appearances of the risen Christ hardened Thomas's skepticism. Finally the moment came for Thomas's doubts to be dispelled:

A week later his disciples were in the house again, and Thomas was with them. Though the doors were locked, Jesus came and stood among them and said, "Peace be with you!" Then he said to Thomas, "Put your finger here; see my hands. Reach out your hand and put it into my side. Stop doubting and believe." (John 20:26-27)

Though Jesus invited Thomas to put his fingers in His hand and His side to authenticate the wounds, we are not told that Thomas actually did so. Perhaps the visual evidence was sufficient for him. Thomas's response was sudden and dramatic: "Thomas said to him, 'My Lord and my God!'" (John 20:28). Thomas' confession is vital to the New Testament record of Jesus. He confessed not only that Jesus was Lord but He clearly ascribed deity to Christ. He called Him "God."

Those who deny the deity of Christ and insist the New Testament does not teach it must contort themselves in pain over this passage. They plead that just because Thomas, in his excitement, gets carried away and calls Jesus "God" does not indicate that this is the teaching of the New Testament. That is a correct observation. It is possible that John merely records Thomas's confession without giving approval to it. That is, however, unlikely.

If John did not want to convey the idea that Thomas'
confession was sound, he would have been quick to add
an editorial disclaimer, as he frequently did editorialize.
Yet John's silence on the matter is nothing compared with
the silence of Jesus. Jesus offered no rebuke to Thomas
for calling Him "God."

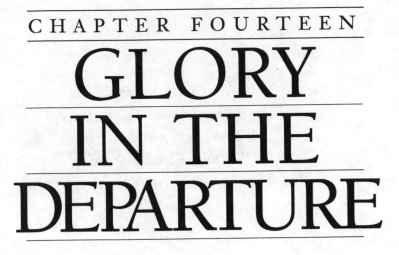

CHAPTER FOURTEEN

GLORY IN THE DEPARTURE

O risen Christ, ascended Lord,
All praise to you let earth accord,
Who are, while endless ages run,
With Father, and with Spirit, One.

THE VENERABLE BEDE

P ROTESTANT CHURCHES celebrate Christmas, Good Friday, and Easter. Some churches also celebrate Pentecost. Yet few Protestant churches give much attention to celebrating the Ascension of Jesus. This probably reflects an inadequate understanding of the importance of this event. In a sense the Ascension is the culmination of the earthly ministry of Jesus and deserves to be ranked as important as Good Friday, Easter, and Pentecost.

These events are linked to one another. Without the cross there is no redemption. And without the Resurrection we would be left with a dead "Savior" whose ability to save would be highly questionable. The Resurrection marks God's stamp of approval upon the sacrifice of Christ. It is unthinkable to have a crucifixion without a Resurrection. As Peter indicated in his sermon on Pentecost, it was impossible that Christ not be raised from the dead. Death had no claim on Him. Therefore death could have no hold on Him:

"Men of Israel, listen to this: Jesus of Nazareth was a man accredited by God to you by miracles, wonders and signs, which God did among you through him, as you yourselves know. This man was handed over to you by God's set purpose and foreknowledge; and you, with the help of wicked men, put him to death by nailing him to the cross. But God raised him from the dead, freeing him from the

agony of death, because it was impossible for death to keep its hold on him. " (Acts 2:22-24)

Just as it is unthinkable to contemplate a crucifixion without a Resurrection, so is it unthinkable to have a Resurrection without an Ascension. If there had been no Ascension, there would not have been a fitting exaltation of Christ. He would have failed to receive the promised glorification by the Father. Without the Ascension, there would be no Pentecost and no Second Coming.

Jesus Himself taught His disciples that the Ascension was a necessary prerequisite for Pentecost to happen:

"Now I am going to him who sent me, yet none of you asks me, 'Where are you going?' Because I have said these things, you are filled with grief. But I tell you the truth: It is for your good that I am going away. Unless I go away, the Counselor will not come to you; but if I go, I will send him to you." (John 16:5-7)

Perhaps our reluctance to celebrate the Ascension of Jesus is rooted in the same problem the disciples struggled with. We are not overjoyed at the absence of Jesus from our midst. Though He promised His abiding presence with us, it is an invisible and intangible presence. We long for His return so that we may delight in His physical presence.

As physical beings we place great value on the physical presence of those whom we hold dear. We use the phrase "out of sight, out of mind" to indicate our failing ardor in the case of absence. The telephone companies assert that long distance calls are "the next best thing to being there." But they are way behind actually being there in person.

The disciples were grieved when Jesus told them that He was going to depart. Jesus rebuked them for failing to ask "Where are you going?" It is the answer to the *where* question as well as the *why* of Jesus' departure that the church of every generation has had difficulty embracing.

Jesus' disciples had trouble grasping the truth that it was to their advantage for Him to leave. If His teaching was true, then it follows that we, who live after His Ascension, share in that advantage.

If we believe what Jesus said to His disciples, we must conclude that we are living in a time that is more advantageous to us than had we been alive during the course of Jesus' earthly ministry. We live post-Ascension and post-Pentecost. The disciples lived during the period of Jesus' humiliation; we live in the period of His exaltation. That is a profound advantage.

THE ASCENSION ACCOUNT

The actual records of Jesus' Ascension are brief in the New Testament. References to it, however, are manifold. Mark describes the Ascension in one sentence (16:19). Luke's Gospel gives but two sentences (24:50-51). Matthew and John give no account at all. The fullest account is in the Book of Acts:

On one occasion, while he was eating with them, he gave them this command: "Do not leave Jerusalem, but wait for

185

*the gift my Father promised, which you have heard me
speak about. For John baptized with water, but in a few
days you will be baptized with the Holy Spirit."*

*So when they met together, they asked him, "Lord, are
you at this time going to restore the kingdom to Israel?"*

*He said to them: "It is not for you to know the times or
dates the Father has set by his own authority. But you will
receive power when the Holy Spirit comes on you; and you
will be my witnesses in Jerusalem, and in all Judea and
Samaria, and to the ends of the earth."*

*After he said this, he was taken up before their very eyes,
and a cloud hid him from their sight.*

*They were looking intently up into the sky as he was
going, when suddenly two men dressed in white stood beside
them. "Men of Galilee," they said, "why do you stand here
looking into the sky? This same Jesus, who has been taken
from you into heaven, will come back in the same way you
have seen him go into heaven."*

*Then they returned to Jerusalem from the hill called
the Mount of Olives, a Sabbath day's walk from the city.*
(Acts 1:4-12)

At the time of His departure Jesus instructed His
disciples to remain in Jerusalem to await the coming of
the Holy Spirit. In their final moments together the
disciples asked their final question of Jesus. They
asked if now was the moment that He intended to
restore the kingdom to Israel. Their question revealed
that they still did not fully understand Jesus' kingship. Jesus did not rebuke them for supposing that He
would at some point restore the kingdom to Israel.
Rather, He told them that it was not for them to know
God's exact timetable. At this point He stressed the
importance of their mission in the interim between

His departure and His return in glory. He told them that they would be empowered to carry out their task during His absence. Their task, and subsequently the task of the Christian church, was to be witnesses to Him.

We will see that the destination of Christ in the Ascension was to His enthronement in heaven. By the Ascension Christ is elevated to the role of cosmic King. His present reign, however, is invisible to the inhabitants of this world. It was the task of His disciples, and now of us, to bear witness to that invisible reign. John Calvin declared that it is the task of the visible church to make the invisible reign of Christ visible to the world. That is the stated purpose of the empowering of the Spirit Jesus promised His people.

The disciples were eyewitnesses of Jesus' departure. As they were watching, He was taken up in a cloud. It is clear from Scripture that the cloud of Ascension was the shekinah glory cloud. Later descriptions of His return in clouds of glory bear that out.

The disciples stood transfixed on the Mount of Olives as they beheld Jesus' glorious departure. Their reverie was interrupted by the presence of angels. The angelic question was almost redundant: "Men of Galilee, why are you standing here gazing into heaven?" These men would surely keep their eyes riveted on this majestic sight as long as any glimpse of the departing glory remained.

The mood of the disciples after Jesus left was dramatically different from the mood they expressed when he first told them that He was going to leave. Now there was no evidence of sorrow. Luke's account underscores their emotional state:

While he was blessing them, he left them and was taken up into heaven. Then they worshiped him and returned to Jerusalem with great joy. (Luke 24:51-52)

Luke here reveals that the disciples were joyful when they returned to Jerusalem. This change in mood is remarkable. When we take leave of our loved ones, especially on occasions when it seems likely that we will never see them again in this world, it is an occasion of great sadness.

How then can we account for the great joy? Perhaps it can be explained in part by the remaining glow they felt from witnessing this manifestation of glory. But that would provide only partial explanation. The full explanation must lie in the change of understanding they experienced. They had come to realize the meaning of Jesus' teaching that it was to their advantage that He depart. Once they grasped the where and the why of the Ascension, they were able to rejoice in the when of His departure.

During Jesus' discourse on the Holy Spirit in the upper room, He uttered words that must have rung in the disciples' ears as they returned from the Mount of Olives:

"You heard me say, 'I am going away and I am coming back to you.' If you loved me, you would be glad that I am going to the Father, for the Father is greater than I. I have told you now before it happens, so that when it does happen you will believe." (John 14:28-29)

188

It is obvious from Luke's account of the disciples' joy that indeed they finally did come to believe Jesus' teaching concerning His departure. Because they did love Him deeply they were able to rejoice that He was ascending to His Father.

THE LEGACY OF JESUS

There is one more element that would have added to the disciples' joy. After Jesus left them, they received the legacy He had promised them. When a wealthy patriarch dies, the mourning of his family is sometimes tempered when the will is read and they receive the inheritance. Sometimes the anticipation of a large inheritance makes children hope for the hasty departure of their parents.

Jesus left no worldly estate. His legacy was of a different kind. He left His disciples His peace, a possession of inestimable worth:

"Peace I leave with you; my peace I give you. I do not give to you as the world gives. Do not let your hearts be troubled and do not be afraid." (John 14:27)

The peace that Jesus left His disciples was not an ordinary peace. Jesus defined it as "my peace." It was a transcendent peace, a peace that passes understanding. It was a peace that has the power to overcome despair. It was the peace for which every Jew longed. It was the supreme blessing of *Shalom.*

Paul indicates that the first benefit derived from the believer's justification is a participation in this peace that includes peace with God: "Therefore, since we have been justified through faith, we have peace with God through our Lord Jesus Christ" (Romans 5:1). Elsewhere the apostle declares: "For he himself is our peace, who has made the two one and has destroyed the barrier, the dividing wall of hostility" (Ephesians 2:14). In leaving His peace as a legacy to His church, Jesus was leaving Himself in His abiding spiritual presence.

THE ENTHRONEMENT OF JESUS

The disciples came to understand that Jesus was returning to His Father. His Ascension, however, did not refer merely to His going "up to heaven." There was a uniqueness that was not shared in by previous people who went to heaven. Jesus ascended in a way Enoch and Elijah, for example, did not. Jesus indicated this in one of His teachings: "No one has ever gone into heaven except the one who came from heaven—the Son of Man" (John 3:13). In His discussion with Nicodemus, Jesus hinted at the uniqueness of His Ascension. Others had gone to heaven, but no one had ascended in the special sense that He would. Only the One who had descended from heaven was qualified to ascend in the special sense of the word. Here the word *ascend* means far more than simply "going up." It has specific reference to going up to a specific place to perform a specific task. Jesus was ascending to where He would be enthroned as the King of kings and Lord of lords. He was being seated at the right hand of the Father in the place of cosmic authority.

190

The Ascension of Jesus marked the fulfillment of Psalm 110:

The LORD says to my Lord:
"Sit at my right hand
until I make your enemies
a footstool for your feet."
The LORD will extend your mighty scepter from Zion;
you will rule in the midst of your enemies.
Your troops will be willing
on your day of battle.
Arrayed in holy majesty,
from the womb of the dawn
you will receive the dew of your youth.
The LORD has sworn
and will not change his mind:
"You are a priest forever,
in the order of Melchizedek."
The Lord is at your right hand;
he will crush kings on the day of his wrath.
He will judge the nations, heaping up the dead
and crushing the rulers of the whole earth.
He will drink from a brook beside the way;
therefore he will lift up his head.

I cite Psalm 110 here because it is Old Testament passage most frequently quoted and alluded to in the New Testament. This psalm incorporates the full measure of the destiny of the Messiah. The royal messiah will be situated at the right hand of God, where He will execute both the office of the God's anointed King and the office of our great High Priest.

That this is fulfilled in the Ascension is clear from Paul's teaching:

191

Therefore God exalted him to the highest place
  and gave him the name that is above every name,
that at the name of Jesus every knee should bow,
  in heaven and on earth and under the earth,
and every tongue confess that Jesus Christ is Lord,
  to the glory of God the Father.

(Philippians 2:9-11)

In His Ascension, Jesus receives both the office and the title of Lord. He enters into His "Session" (meaning, His "seating") at the right hand of God. This is the position of glory, honor, dominion, and power. It is the subject of the song of the angels in Revelation:

Then I looked and heard the voice of many angels, numbering thousands upon thousands, and ten thousand times ten thousand. They encircled the throne and the living creatures and the elders. In a loud voice they sang:

"Worthy is the Lamb, who was slain,
to receive power and wealth and wisdom and strength
  and honor and glory and praise!"

  Then I heard every creature in heaven and on earth and under the earth and on the sea, and all that is in them, singing:

"To him who sits on the throne and to the Lamb
be praise and honor and glory and power,
  for ever and ever!"

The four living creatures said, "Amen," and the elders fell down and worshiped. (Revelation 5:11-14)

The Ascension was a central point of the *kerygma*, the proclamation of the apostolic preaching. We note its presence in Peter's sermon on Pentecost:

"God has raised this Jesus to life, and we are all witnesses of the fact. Exalted to the right hand of God, he has received

192

from the Father the promised Holy Spirit and has poured out
what you now see and hear. For David did not ascend to
heaven, and yet he said,
'*The Lord said to my Lord:*
  "*Sit at my right hand*
until I make your enemies
  a footstool for your feet."'
  Therefore let all Israel be assured of this: God has made
this Jesus, whom you crucified, both Lord and Christ."
(Acts 2:32-36)

CHRIST'S ROLE OF INTERCESSION

In the Ascension, Jesus not only assumed the role of
King but also that of the High Priest forever after the
order of Melchizedek. We have seen the record of Jesus'
prayer of intercession in the upper room. It is important
to realize that this work of intercession continues even
to this day. This theme of Jesus' heavenly ministry as
our High Priest is discussed at length in Hebrews:

Since we have a great high priest who has gone through
the heavens, Jesus the Son of God, let us hold firmly to the
faith we profess. For we do not have a high priest who is
unable to sympathize with our weaknesses, but we have one
who has been tempted in every way, just as we are—yet
was without sin. Let us then approach the throne of grace
with confidence, so that we may receive mercy and find
grace to help us in our time of need. (Hebrews 4:14-16)

The scope of Christ's priestly work is of vast importance to us. His work as High Priest is perpetual.

Because Jesus lives forever, he has a permanent priesthood.
Therefore he is able to save completely those who come to

193

God through him, because he always lives to intercede for them.

Such a high priest meets our need—one who is holy, blameless, pure, set apart from sinners, exalted above the heavens. Unlike the other high priests, he does not need to offer sacrifices day after day, first for his own sins, and then for the sins of the people. He sacrificed for their sins once for all when he offered himself. For the law appoints as high priests men who are weak; but the oath, which came after the law, appointed the Son, who has been made perfect forever. The point of what we are saying is this: We do have such a high priest, who sat down at the right hand of the throne of the Majesty in heaven, and who serves in the sanctuary, the true tabernacle set up by the Lord, not by man. (Hebrews 2:14–8:2)

JESUS AS OUR ADVOCATE

In His heavenly role as the King-Priest, Jesus serves as our defense attorney. Though when the Bible speaks of Jesus in His ascended glory as normally being seated at the right hand of God, there are occasions when He rises from that seat to speak in the defense of His saints. We see this in the closing moments of Stephen's life.

Stephen had preached a scathing sermon of judgment before the Jewish authorities. Their reaction was one of fury; they were cut to the heart and gnashed their teeth at him. In the midst of this crisis, as Stephen fell under the judgment of the highest Jewish tribunal of this world, he looked into glory itself:

But Stephen, full of the Holy Spirit, looked up to heaven and saw the glory of God, and Jesus standing at the right hand of God. "Look," he said, "I see heaven open and the Son of Man standing at the right hand of God." (Acts 7:55–56)

Stephen saw Jesus "standing" at the right hand of God. In the courtroom only two people stand, the prosecuting attorney and the defense attorney. The judge remains seated at the bench. In His role of Son of Man and ascended Lord, Jesus is seated in the place of rule and of judgment. On this occasion, however, the divine judge rises from the bench and assumes the role of defense attorney.

This is the role Jesus performs not only for Stephen but for all of His people. At the Last Judgment we may be assured that our judge will also serve as our defense attorney. He is our Advocate with the Father.

THE ASCENSION AND PENTECOST

Jesus described a necessary connection between His Ascension to the right hand of the Father and the sending of the Holy Spirit upon the church. Since this book concerns the glory of Jesus as distinguished from the glory of the Holy Ghost we will touch but lightly on the events of Pentecost. (For further discussion of the Spirit, see my book *The Mystery of the Holy Spirit*.)

When the day of Pentecost came, they were all together in one place. Suddenly a sound like the blowing of a violent wind came from heaven and filled the whole house where they were sitting. They saw what seemed to be tongues of fire that separated and came to rest on each of them. All of them were filled with the Holy Spirit and began to speak in other tongues as the Spirit enabled them. (Acts 2:1–4)

There was clearly a display of divine glory at Pentecost. The first manifestation was one of sound. The sound is described as that of a rushing wind. That this wind was no ordinary wind was apparent to those who heard it. The link between wind and Spirit goes deep into the roots of Jewish and Christian religion. Both in the Hebrew language and in the Greek language the word for "spirit" is also the word for "wind" (*ruach* in Hebrew, *pneuma* in Greek). We remember the saying of Jesus when He discussed the power of the Spirit in regeneration:

The wind blows wherever it pleases. You hear its sound, but you cannot tell where it comes from or where it is going. So it is with everyone born of the Spirit. (John 3:8)

Jesus speaks of the freedom by which the wind blows. The Spirit is not controlled by men or by natural forces. The Holy Spirit works according to the sovereign freedom of God. We can hear the wind blowing, but we can neither control its origin nor its destination. So the wind that blew in a violent way at Pentecost manifested the power and the glory of the presence of the Holy Spirit.

The second manifestation of the coming of the Holy Spirit was a visible phenomenon. Those assembled saw tongues of fire resting over each person's head. The tongues of fire signified the resting of divine glory on the place. As the dove visibly descended from heaven and rested on Jesus at His baptism, so now the Spirit rests upon His people. We see here a parallel to the Old Testament account of what happened when the

Spirit that rested with Moses was distributed among the seventy elders:

Then the LORD came down in the cloud and spoke with him, and he took of the Spirit that was on him and put the Spirit on the seventy elders. When the Spirit rested on them, they prophesied, but they did not do so again.
(Numbers 11:25)

The third manifestation of the descent of the Holy Spirit was the speaking in tongues. There is a difficulty in discerning whether this miraculous outbreak was a miracle of speech or a miracle of hearing. Perhaps it involved both. It was the Holy Spirit who was said to give utterance. However, the speech that was uttered was heard variously by those present in their own languages. We are left with the question, Were people given an ability to speak foreign languages, or was there a supernatural work of translation here? It sounds like what happens in the United Nations chambers when foreign dignitaries give their speeches—those listening hear in their earphone a simultaneous translation of the speakers' words:

Now there were staying in Jerusalem God-fearing Jews from every nation under heaven. When they heard this sound, a crowd came together in bewilderment, because each one heard them speaking in his own language. Utterly amazed, they asked: "Are not all these men who are speaking Galileans? Then how is it that each of us hears them in his own native language? Parthians, Medes and Elamites; residents of Mesopotamia, Judea and Cappadocia, Pontus and Asia, Phrygia and Pamphylia, Egypt and the parts of Libya near Cyrene; visitors from

Rome (both Jews and converts to Judaism); Cretans and Arabs—we hear them declaring the wonders of God in our own tongues!" Amazed and perplexed, they asked one another, "What does this mean?" (Acts 2:5-10)

Those present were perplexed. Peter then arose and preached a sermon in which he provided a historical interpretation of the event. He explained the phenomenon of Pentecost as a result of the exaltation of Christ in His Ascension:

"God has raised this Jesus to life, and we are all witnesses of the fact. Exalted to the right hand of God, he has received from the Father the promised Holy Spirit and has poured out what you now see and hear." (Acts 2:32-33)

The sound-and-sight display of Pentecost was the visible manifestation of the glorious outpouring of the Holy Spirit that Jesus had promised His church.

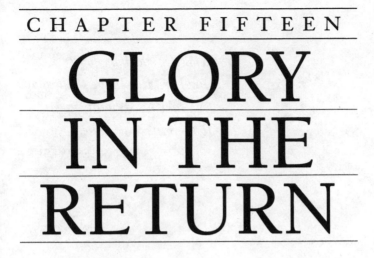

CHAPTER FIFTEEN

GLORY IN THE RETURN

Rejoice in glorious hope!
Our Lord the Judge shall come
And take his servants up
To their eternal home.

CHARLES WESLEY

NONE OF US were eyewitnesses of any of the manifestations of the glory of Christ that we have studied so far. They all occurred centuries ago in faraway Palestine. The audiences of these breakthroughs of splendor were small groups of people. But the most magnificent display of glory is yet to happen. When it does occur, it will be witnessed by billions. Though the first advent was accompanied by a small glimpse of glory, the second will be attended by glory in cosmic proportions.

Visible signs that will accompany Jesus' return are mentioned in the Olivet Discourse. In this discussion with His disciples He made predictions about the destruction of Jerusalem, which occurred in A.D. 70. He coupled this with further information about His final return:

"For as lightning that comes from the east is visible even in the west, so will be the coming of the Son of Man. Wherever there is a carcass, there the vultures will gather.

Immediately after the distress of those days
'the sun will be darkened,
and the moon will not give its light;
the stars will fall from the sky,
and the heavenly bodies will be shaken.'

At that time the sign of the Son of Man will appear in the sky, and all the nations of the earth will mourn. They will see the Son of Man coming on the clouds of the sky, with power and great glory. And he will send his angels with a loud trumpet call, and they will gather his elect from the four winds, from one end of the heavens to the other." (Matthew 24:27-31)

The phenomena that will take place in the sky at the time of Christ's return are described with images borrowed from the Old Testament. The day of the Lord prophesied in the Old Testament parallels many of these images:

Before them the earth shakes,
  the sky trembles,
the sun and moon are darkened,
  and the stars no longer shine.
The LORD thunders
  at the head of his army;
his forces are beyond number,
  and mighty are those who obey his command.
The day of the LORD is great;
  it is dreadful.
  Who can endure it?

(Joel 2:10-11)

For those who persist in unbelief, the day of Christ's coming will be a time of great mourning. But for those who love Him, it will be a time of glory. Again the clouds of glory will be the vehicle of His transportation.

The appearance of Christ will be also heralded by heavenly sounds:

For the Lord himself will come down from heaven, with a loud command, with the voice of the archangel and with the trumpet call of God, and the dead in Christ will rise first. After that, we who are still alive and are left will be caught up together with them in the clouds to meet the

Lord in the air. And so we will be with the Lord forever.
(1 Thessalonians 4:16-17)

The sounds of the coming of Christ will include a "loud command," the voice of an archangel, and the trumpet call of God—sounds characteristic of a blaring announcement. It will be as if a celestial loudspeaker calls the earth to attention. As the *shophar,* the ram's horn, was blown in Old Testament Israel to summon the nation to solemn assembly and as trumpets were used by Roman warriors to summon the troops to battle, so the earth will hear an announcement from on high to signal the entrance of Christ the King.

Some people believe that the return of Christ will involve a secret Rapture of the saints. (This theory involves *two* distinct returns of Christ.) The Bible indicates, however, that His appearance will be the worst kept secret in history. It will be a public appearance heralded by astronomic wonders and a glorious heralding from the realm of glory itself.

Paul warns that the coming of Christ will be unexpected: "for you know very well that the day of the Lord will come like a thief in the night" (1 Thessalonians 5:2). This image is also used by Peter:

But the day of the Lord will come like a thief. The heavens will disappear with a roar; the elements will be destroyed by fire, and the earth and everything in it will be laid bare.
(2 Peter 3:10)

The image of the thief has been used to support the notion of Jesus' secret coming. But in Peter's letter the image is accompanied by a description of the roar of the heavens and other cataclysmic effects. Both in Peter's and Paul's use of the image of the thief, the analogy is not one that stresses silence or secretness, but *suddenness*. The thief is unexpected.

The unexpectedness has to do with the attitude of unbelievers. To them it will be a thief in the night. When the thief comes, however, he will trip an alarm that will awaken the entire neighborhood.

That Peter has in view the unbelieving world as the ones who will suffer the shock of surprise is seen by the immediate context of his teaching:

You must understand that in the last days scoffers will come, scoffing and following their own evil desires. They will say, "Where is this 'coming' he promised? Ever since our fathers died, everything goes on as it has since the beginning of creation." But they deliberately forget that long ago by God's word the heavens existed and the earth was formed out of water and by water. By these waters also the world of that time was deluged and destroyed. By the same word the present heavens and earth are reserved for fire, being kept for the day of judgment and destruction of ungodly men.

But do not forget this one thing, dear friends: With the Lord a day is like a thousand years, and a thousand years are like a day. The Lord is not slow in keeping his promise, as some understand slowness. He is patient with you, not wanting anyone to perish, but everyone to come to repentance.

But the day of the Lord will come like a thief. The heavens will disappear with a roar; the elements will be destroyed by fire, and the earth and everything in it will be laid bare. (2 Peter 3:3-10)

It is the scoffers who will experience the sudden coming of Jesus as a thief in the night. Likewise, in Paul's use of the image he indicates that though His coming will involve surprise to some, it is not to come unawares to the vigilant believer:

While people are saying, "Peace and safety," destruction will come on them suddenly, as labor pains on a pregnant woman, and they will not escape.

But you, brothers, are not in darkness so that this day should surprise you like a thief. You are all sons of the light and sons of the day. We do not belong to the night or to the darkness. So then, let us not be like others, who are asleep, but let us be alert and self-controlled. (1 Thessalonians 5:3-8)

Those who are of the darkness are caught in their sleep by the thief in the night. We are to be numbered among those who are not surprised.

THE RAPTURE OF THE SAINTS

The Rapture refers to believers being caught up in the air to meet Christ when He comes. Those who believe in a "secret" Rapture and two distinct comings of Christ view the Rapture as an event in which the church will be taken out of the world and joined with Jesus at His first coming. They will then abide with Jesus for a time until He returns the second time for judgment.

This view is based on a questionable interpretation of one Scripture passage:

Don't let anyone deceive you in any way, for that day will not come until the rebellion occurs and the man of lawlessness is revealed, the man doomed to destruction. He

*will oppose and will exalt himself over everything that is
called God or is worshiped, so that he sets himself up in
God's temple, proclaiming himself to be God.*

*Don't you remember that when I was with you I used to
tell you these things? And now you know what is holding
him back, so that he may be revealed at the proper time.
For the secret power of lawlessness is already at work; but
the one who now holds it back will continue to do so till he
is taken out of the way. And then the lawless one will be
revealed, whom the Lord Jesus will overthrow with the
breath of his mouth and destroy by the splendor of his
coming. The coming of the lawless one will be in accordance
with the work of Satan displayed in all kinds of counterfeit
miracles, signs and wonders, and in every sort of evil that
deceives those who are perishing. They perish because they
refused to love the truth and so be saved. For this reason
God sends them a powerful delusion so that they will
believe the lie and so that all will be condemned who have
not believed the truth but have delighted in wickedness.*
(2 Thessalonians 2:3-12)

This portion of Paul's teaching focuses upon the manifestation of the man of lawlessness, who, Paul insists,
must appear before the coming of Christ. His appearance marks the beginning of a time of severe tribulation. Those who teach a pre-tribulation Rapture insist
that the saints will not have to endure this difficult time.
They will be taken away (raptured) before the man of
lawlessness is set loose on earth.

The key concept in this view is the removal of the
restraints from the man of lawlessness. The understanding of verses 6 and 7 are important. The question focuses
on the identity of the "restrainer" who must be taken out
of the way before the man of lawlessness can usher in the

tribulation. In the speculation of a pre-tribulation Rapture the one who restrains is interpreted to be the Holy Spirit. The reasoning goes like this: The Holy Spirit is the restrainer of the man of lawlessness, and the restrainer must be removed for the tribulation to occur; since the Holy Spirit indwells every believer, the only way to remove the restrainer is to remove all believers from the earth. So it follows that Christians will all be removed before the man of lawlessness appears.

Since Paul explicitly teaches here that the day of the Lord will not come until the man of sin comes, it is necessary for those who hold to a pre-tribulation Rapture to conclude that Jesus must come twice—first to Rapture His church and then to usher in the day of the Lord. The effect of this theory is to annul the very purpose for the apostolic teaching. Paul is urging his readers not to be deceived by teaching that suggests that Christ will come before the appearance of the man of lawlessness. Paul's teaching here is brutalized by those who postulate an unbiblical divorce between the day of the Lord and the coming (*parousia*) of Christ. What God has joined together, this theory puts asunder.

The Bible does not identify the restrainer as the Holy Spirit. Even if the restrainer is the Holy Spirit, for God to cease His role of restraint would not necessitate the cessation of His presence altogether by removing believers from the world.

The significance of the Rapture is not that it will remove the church from the world during the tribulation. The whole point of the Rapture is the privilege given to the church to meet their arriving King and be part of His entourage. The point is that we will participate with Jesus in His coming in glory.

Paul's imagery for the Rapture is borrowed from events that were well-known in his day. The phenomenon of joining in triumphal procession of the victor was played out frequently by the Roman armies. To this day, at places around the globe that once belonged to the Roman Empire, we still find evidence standing of their military practice. The monuments to Roman conquests that still stand are the magnificent arches, such as the Arch of Titus.

When Roman legions returned to Rome after victorious forays, they did not enter the city immediately. Instead, they camped about a mile outside the city until the city was made ready for a triumphal march into it. The streets of the city were adorned with garlands, and an arch of triumph was built. Sweet aromas were also spread in the path of the march to conceal the stench of the prisoners who were paraded in their bonds. Once all was ready, the signal for the procession to begin was the blowing of trumpets. At that signal the citizens of Rome (not all of its inhabitants) were invited to march with the conquering army as part of their victorious entourage. Atop the banners held aloft by the legionnaires was the insignia SPQR, initials which, in Latin, stood for "For the Senate and the People of Rome." The army was seen as an embodiment of the citizenry of Rome. So the citizens participated in the triumph.

After the citizens went out to the camp, the parade

lines were formed. The procession entered the city through the arch, leading captives in chains, as Jesus was said to "lead captivity captive." The point of the imagery of the Rapture is one of participation. The saints are taken up in the air—not to disappear or to hover there during the tribulation, but to be included in the entourage of the King. This is the fulfillment of the frequent biblical promises that we shall share in the exaltation of Christ.

The entire company of saints will participate in this decisive manifestation of the glory of Jesus. Not only those living at the time of His return, but all saints, living and dead, will share in the moment.

Paul's concern in 1 Thessalonians is to dispel any idea that those who die before the triumphant return of Jesus will miss that event. He provides assurance that all Christians will be eyewitnesses of this cosmic spectacle:

Brothers, we do not want you to be ignorant about those who fall asleep, or to grieve like the rest of men, who have no hope. We believe that Jesus died and rose again and so we believe that God will bring with Jesus those who have fallen asleep in him. According to the Lord's own word, we tell you that we who are still alive, who are left till the coming of the Lord, will certainly not precede those who have fallen asleep. For the Lord himself will come down from heaven, with a loud command, with the voice of the archangel and with the trumpet call of God, and the dead in Christ will rise first. After that, we who are still alive and are left will be caught up together with them in the clouds to meet the Lord in the air. And so we will be with the Lord forever. Therefore encourage each other with these words. (1 Thessalonians 4:13-18)

Indeed, these words from the apostle bring comfort to the hearts of believers. The comfort comes from the certainty that we will see and hear the consummate manifestation of the glory of our Lord. That moment will fulfill what Paul wrote elsewhere:

As it is written:
"No eye has seen, no ear has heard, no mind has conceived what God has prepared for those who love him."
(1 Corinthians 2:9)

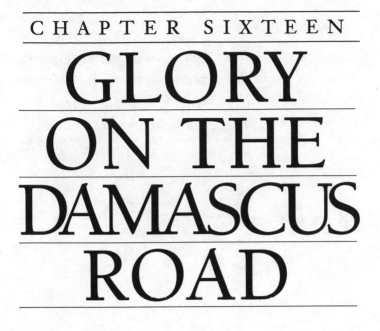

CHAPTER SIXTEEN

GLORY ON THE DAMASCUS ROAD

God's light shone down from heaven
And broke across the path.
His presence pierced and blinded
The zealot in his wrath.

JOHN ELLERTON

A**S WE CONSIDER** the breakthroughs of the glory of Jesus, it is important to understand the effects they had on those who were present. This is nowhere more profound than in the case of Saul of Tarsus.

Saul was still breathing out murderous threats against the Lord's disciples. He went to the high priest and asked him for letters to the synagogues in Damascus, so that if he found any there who belonged to the Way, whether men or women, he might take them as prisoners to Jerusalem. (Acts 9:1-2)

Saul was zealous for traditional Judaism. He had distinguished himself as a student under the famous Rabbi Gamaliel. He later described himself as a Pharisee of Pharisees. His zeal for tradition was coupled with a loathing for the new Jewish sect called "People of the Way," people who declared that Jesus was the Messiah.

Saul was not exactly an objective investigator. Luke described him as one who "breathed out threats" and murder against the Christians. He had been a party to the stoning of Stephen:

Saul was there, giving approval to his [Stephen's] death. On that day a great persecution broke out against the church at Jerusalem, and all except the apostles were scattered throughout Judea and Samaria. Godly men buried Stephen and mourned deeply for him. But Saul began to destroy the church. Going from house to house, he dragged off men and women and put them in prison. (Acts 8:1-3)

Saul pursued his persecution with unswerving intensity, seeking permission to carry his crusade as far as Damascus. His trip on the desert road was interrupted by a bursting forth of the glory of Christ: "As he neared Damascus on his journey, suddenly a light from heaven flashed around him" (Acts 9:3). Paul later recounted this vision in his defense before King Agrippa:

"I too was convinced that I ought to do all that was possible to oppose the name of Jesus of Nazareth . . . . On the authority of the chief priests I put many of the saints in prison, and when they were put to death, I cast my vote against them. Many a time I went from one synagogue to another to have them punished, and I tried to force them to blaspheme. In my obsession against them, I even went to foreign cities to persecute them.

"On one of these journeys I was going to Damascus with the authority and commission of the chief priests. About noon, O king, as I was on the road, I saw a light from heaven, brighter than the sun, blazing around me and my companions." (Acts 26:9-13)

The appearance of Christ to Saul took place after Jesus' Ascension. It was a special visitation to effect the conversion of Saul, the one who would be the apostle to the Gentiles. The appearance of Christ was signaled by the blaze of light, indicating divine glory. Paul later counted this among the visible manifestations of the proof of the Resurrection of Jesus:

. . . that he was buried, that he was raised on the third day according to the Scriptures, and that he appeared to Peter, and then to the Twelve. After that, he appeared to more than five hundred of the brothers at the same time, most of whom are still living, though some have fallen

asleep. Then he appeared to James, then to all the apostles, and last of all he appeared to me also, as to one abnormally born.

For I am the least of the apostles and do not even deserve to be called an apostle, because I persecuted the church of God. (1 Corinthians 15:4-9)

When Paul saw the blazing light from heaven, he fell to the ground. Immediately he heard the audible voice of Christ: "Saul, Saul, why do you persecute me?" (Acts 9:4). Two things are noteworthy about these words. The first is the repeated form of address. It is rare in Scripture when people are addressed by the repeated form of their name. As God addressed Abraham at Mount Moriah ("Abraham, Abraham"), Moses from the burning bush ("Moses, Moses"), and others, so Jesus on occasion addressed people by repeating their names. He spoke in this manner to Martha, to Simon, to the Father from the cross, to the city of Jerusalem in His lament, and now to Saul. It is a form of address that suggests respect as well as intimacy.

It seems out of character for Jesus to address Saul in this manner, given the fact that Saul was Enemy Number One for the church. But Jesus in His mercy addressed Saul in this manner.

The second important element of Jesus' words to Saul is the query, "Why are you persecuting me?" Jesus did not ask Saul why he was persecuting His church. A persecution of His church was a persecution of Himself. To attack His people is to attack Him.

When Saul heard these words, his immediate response was to ask for the identity of the One who was speaking to him: "'Who are you, Lord?' Saul asked. 'I am Jesus, whom you are persecuting,' he replied" (Acts 9:5). We notice here that though Saul did not immediately realize whom he was speaking with, he at least recognized that whoever it was, was Lord. Saul understood that he was in the presence of divine majesty.

In his defense before Agrippa, Paul added the detail that Jesus then added "It is hard for you to kick against the goads" (Acts 26:14).

To "kick against the goads" was to behave like a stupid ox. The oxgoad was a thick board attached to carts drawn by oxen. The board had sharp spikes pointed in the direction of the animals. If the oxen became stubborn and refused to move forward, the goad was used to prod them on. At times the stubborn oxen would kick backwards against the goad, inflicting severe pain upon themselves. The more pain they experienced, the harder they would kick.

Saul's furious rage against the Christian church resulted in his inflicting damage to his own soul. The more he raged against Christ, the deeper in trouble he was. He was, like the oxen, fighting a losing battle. His fury was no match for the strength and power of Christ. Now as Saul confronts his adversary in the splendor of His majesty, he knows that he has been defeated.

Saul's transformation into the apostle Paul was a matter of sheer sovereign grace. The glory that Jesus revealed to Saul was withheld from Pilate and Caiaphas. There was no merit to which Saul could point as the reason for this visitation of grace. Paul, by his own testimony, was the chief of sinners. Christ did not wait for Saul to repent or otherwise incline his soul toward Christ before He manifested Himself to him. Let others argue about the doctrine of irresistible grace. Paul did not debate it. He was redeemed by it. He knew that the grace he received in that hour was completely unmerited and was, to him, irresistible.

As a result of this encounter, Saul was struck blind. There is among men a blindness to the glory of Christ. Paul's was a blindness *from* the glory of Christ.

Having identified Himself, Jesus continued:

"Now get up and go into the city, and you will be told what you must do."

The men traveling with Saul stood there speechless; they heard the sound but did not see anyone. Saul got up from the ground, but when he opened his eyes he could see nothing. So they led him by the hand into Damascus. For three days he was blind, and did not eat or drink anything. (Acts 9:6-9)

Following this, the Lord appeared to Ananias and gave instructions for the healing of Saul:

In Damascus there was a disciple named Ananias. The Lord called to him in a vision, "Ananias!"

"Yes, Lord," he answered.

The Lord told him, "Go to the house of Judas on Straight Street and ask for a man from Tarsus named Saul, for he is praying. In a vision he has seen a man named Ananias come and place his hands on him to restore his sight."

"Lord," Ananias answered, "I have heard many reports about this man and all the harm he has done to your saints

217

in Jerusalem. And he has come here with authority from the chief priests to arrest all who call on your name."

But the Lord said to Ananias, "Go! This man is my chosen instrument to carry my name before the Gentiles and their kings and before the people of Israel. I will show him how much he must suffer for my name."

Then Ananias went to the house and entered it. Placing his hands on Saul, he said, "Brother Saul, the Lord—Jesus, who appeared to you on the road as you were coming here—has sent me so that you may see again and be filled with the Holy Spirit." Immediately, something like scales fell from Saul's eyes, and he could see again. He got up and was baptized, and after taking some food, he regained his strength. Saul spent several days with the disciples in Damascus. (Acts 9:10-19)

In His instructions to Ananias, Christ stated that Paul was His chosen instrument. He had selected Paul to be chief witness to the Gentiles. When Ananias laid his hands on Saul, his sight was restored. He was filled with the Holy Spirit and empowered for the ministry that lay ahead.

When Paul later recounted these things to King Agrippa, he made a bold but sober statement of truth:

"'Now get up and stand on your feet. I have appeared to you to appoint you as a servant and as a witness of what you have seen of me and what I will show you. I will rescue you from your own people and from the Gentiles. I am sending you to them to open their eyes and turn them from darkness to light, and from the power of Satan to God, so that they may receive forgiveness of sins and a place among those who are sanctified by faith in me.'

So then, King Agrippa, I was not disobedient to the vision from heaven." (Acts 26:16-19)

After Paul recounted to the king his conversion experience and his commission to apostleship he declared, "I was not disobedient to the vision from heaven." This is the statement every Christian longs to make at the end of his life. This is the proper response to the manifestation of the glory of Christ.